RUSTIC GARDEN FURNITURE
& ACCESSORIES

RUSTIC GARDEN FURNITURE
& ACCESSORIES

Making Chairs, Planters, Birdhouses, Gates & More

Daniel Mack &
Thomas Stender

LARK BOOKS
A Division of Sterling Publishing Co., Inc.
New York

EXECUTIVE EDITOR
Deborah Morgenthal

COPY EDITOR
Kathy Sheldon

ART DIRECTOR
Celia Naranjo

PRODUCTION
Charlie Covington

COVER DESIGNER
Barbara Zaretsky

ILLUSTRATOR
Frank Rohrbach

ASSOCIATE ART DIRECTOR
Shannon Yokeley

EDITORIAL ASSISTANCE
Delores Gosnell
Veronika Gunter

The Library of Congress has cataloged the hardcover edition as follows:

Mack, Daniel.
  Rustic garden furniture & accessories : making chairs, planters, birdhouses, gates & more / by Daniel Mack and Thomas Stender.
       p. cm.
           Includes index.
    ISBN 1-57990-355-X (hardcover)
1. Outdoor furniture--Design and construction. 2. Garden ornaments and furniture--Design and construction. 3. Woodwork. I. Title: Rustic garden furniture and accessories. II. Stender, Thomas. III. Title.
TT197.5.O9M33 2004
684.1'8--dc22

                              2003021993

10 9 8 7 6 5 4 3 2 1

Published by Lark Books, A Division of
Sterling Publishing Co., Inc.
387 Park Avenue South, New York, N.Y. 10016

First Paperback Edition 2007
© 2004, Daniel Mack and Thomas Stender

Distributed in Canada by Sterling Publishing,
c/o Canadian Manda Group, 165 Dufferin Street
Toronto, Ontario, Canada M6K 3H6

Distributed in the United Kingdom by GMC Distribution Services,
Castle Place, 166 High Street, Lewes, East Sussex, England BN7 1XU

Distributed in Australia by Capricorn Link (Australia) Pty Ltd.,
P.O. Box 704, Windsor, NSW 2756 Australia

If you have questions or comments about this book, please contact:
Lark Books
67 Broadway
Asheville, NC 28801
(828) 253-0467

Manufactured in China

ISBN 13: 978-1-57990-355-8 (hardcover) 978-1-60059-137-2 (paperback)
ISBN 10: 1-57990-355-x (hardcover) 1-60059-137-x (paperback)

For information about custom editions, special sales, premium and corporate purchases, please contact Sterling Special Sales Department at 800-805-5489 or specialsales@sterlingpub.com.

TABLE OF CONTENTS

INTRODUCTION
By Daniel Mack

Rustic woodworking has never been more important. It offers simple pleasures in a complex world. It reconnects people to nature. It exercises the imagination. It encourages the act of making with a very few basic tools and techniques. In short, it's a tonic to weary, 21st century citizens. It helps them slow down, behave in a playful, seemingly inefficient way. What a service!

Rustic woodworking is a connection to the organic nature of life. No two sticks are quite the same. You can't quite predict what the out-come of a rustic project will be. Sometimes things break. Sometimes there are bugs...and we're not talking computers here.

Rustic woodworking is a form of time traveling. It sweeps us back to the past, to other times filled with pioneers, mountain men, voyageurs, bricoleurs, and bodgers. We're initiated into the world of putting things together. We amuse ourselves with the ingenuity we've discovered as we make something rustic.

Rustic projects also impel us into the future. Those twiggy benches and chairs, that fence, may outlast their maker and stand as a testament that someone, sometime did this. They may be discovered and appreciated by a grandchild or just an early bird at a yard sale.

But this isn't just a backwards or forwards time journey. Doing rustic work, here and now, witnesses for others that it's okay to play, okay to tinker, invent, and dabble. In this way, rustic woodworking is a vacation for the professional or home woodworker. So much of contemporary woodworking is technical, calling on the machinist and the plant manager parts of us. Rustic is about approximation—getting things near enough and good enough. These are rare characteristics to encounter in an ever more precise and exacting world. "Going rustic," once in a while, helps to re-balance one's spirit.

So, welcome to this book. No matter what your level of skill or interest, whether you have lots of time or just bits here and there, this generous and wide-ranging collection of projects will guide you into a world of satisfaction.

INTRODUCTION

By Thomas Stender

I have admired rustic furniture for a long time. I remember the first time I saw Dan Mack's chairs. Their elegance spoke of the choices he had made, each one thoughtful and sure and just right, so persuasive that it seemed they could be no other way, even though I knew there were many other sticks in the forest. The chairs supported ideas, too, as well as people. They communicated reverence and remembrance. They had wit, intelligence, and an ironic presence born of being brought, not just indoors, but into an art gallery. And I enjoyed the seeming ad hoc character of his work. To be honest, I envied Dan for having found a way of working so flexibly with wood.

Woodworking in the conventional way is by nature conservative—we must know beforehand precisely what the end product will be, or we will surely make a mess of it in the building. Rustic work thrives on discoveries made in the process, which makes it seem radical and a little threatening to a high-style cabinetmaker. I keep trying to work with wood in a way more akin to ceramics, where important choices can be delayed and even reversed in midstream, and I have made some headway. But I am given to making furniture that conveys simple ideas by horrifically difficult means. Dan and I have shown our work side by side in galleries several times, and the contrasts and similarities have

amused us. That the two bodies of furniture were able to establish a lively conversation honored us both, in my view.

So I was excited when asked to participate in this book. I brought the curiosity and wonder of a partial outsider, and I have written with a similarly situated reader in mind. This book assumes a certain familiarity with tools, some experience with building in wood, and an openness to the discoveries, large and small, that rustic work provides with such generosity. Read and build in that spirit. I know you'll be rewarded.

Camp under construction, Adirondacks, late 19th century

A SHORT HISTORY OF OUTDOOR RUSTIC WORK

By Daniel Mack

It was about 25 years ago that rustic work resurfaced in American popular culture. Actually, it had never left, but it had been eclipsed by various high styles and technologically inventive forms of furniture: slick, smooth, metal, leather, art furniture. So, rough old rustic came back as the country alternative. It was touted as "bringing the outdoors in." Antique rustic pieces, humble old porch chairs, and survivors from the backyard became a part of a visually rich eclec-

tic mix of interior style. It was called American Country, the Santa Fe Look, Neo-Primitive, the Rustic Revival. And a generation of new rustic makers began to invent themselves at craft shows, flea markets, county fairs, garden centers, and in furniture stores and galleries.

Slowly, over the last few decades, rustic has moved back outdoors to its modest origins, into the backyard, the garden, the porch. The surge of interest in gardening has renewed interest in outdoor rustic work. So rustic makers (of which there are an ever-growing number) are now challenged to create furniture and structures that fit into the garden lifestyle that has become such an important part of American life. That's what this book is about.

Rustic first appeared in England in the mid-18th century, as exotic an import as silk, tea, and porcelain. It was welcomed into the English garden and even interpreted in some of the high-style furniture of the day. Certainly Thomas Chippendale's branch-like backs are cousins of actual branches.

Some of the early English rustic style was called "root work" and was related to the Chinese style of using the gnarled, earthy roots as the central motif in rustic structures and furniture. The other major English form of rustic was "forest" or branch work, a highly crafted effort that used tree parts in place of milled lumber. That formula still describes much of the rustic furniture of today—imposing order on otherwise crooked pieces of tree. The wonder of rustic work is that no two makers ever

Barry and Darlene Gregson's first shop, 1986. Photo by Daniel Mack

agree on just how much order should reign or just how crooked the branches can be. This makes for near-endless variation and pleasure in making and living with rustic work.

Before the middle of the 19th century, America was just too young and too wild a country to need or appreciate a style called "rustic." Indeed, the forests, the woods, and nature itself were regarded as overpowering and dangerous forces, harboring enemies and fostering lunacy. The frontier was wide open, and even the log cabin, which came to be the icon of American rustic, was just a form of fast, temporary housing introduced by Northern European immigrants: the Swedes, Finns, and Russians.

Drawing by Matthew Darly of a Chinese-inspired chair, 1784

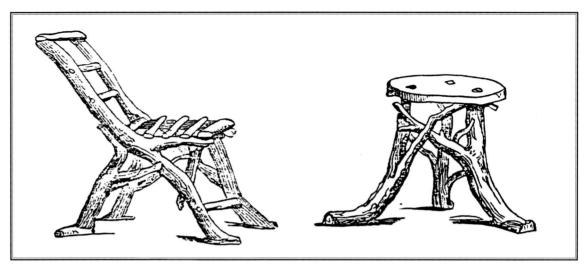

Drawings from "First Article on Rustic Furniture," The Horticulturist, *1858, p.304.*

The wealthy in America, including many of the founding fathers, owned large estates that they groomed in the style of English or Continental gardens with some few minor rustic touches. But it wasn't until 1841, when the American-born landscape designer Andrew Jackson Downing published two important books (*Cottage Residences* and *Treatise on the Theory and Practice of Landscape Gardening*), that the natural and rustic came to be regarded as beautiful. Downing also edited *The Horticulturist*, what we would call a "shelter" magazine today, filled with information, advice, drawings, and budgets for all kinds of home-related projects.

When rustic did catch on, starting in the 1850s, it was heartily embraced as an American idiom. This rustic structure was made at ex-president Ulysses Grant's Michigan farm, which later became the Busch Estate.

Andrew Jackson Downing also became partners with a European-trained architect, Calvert Vaux, who went on, after Downing's untimely death at age 38, to design and build Central Park with Frederick Law Olmsted. These two were responsible for the introduction of rustic into the parks of many major American cities. Their rule of thumb was to create a park that was an anti-city. Where the City was a flat grid of straight streets and tall buildings, the Park contained hilly greenswards with meandering paths, lanes and "rambles" leading to shaggy rustic structures.

Craig Gilborn, the Adirondack historian, believes that the rustic structures of Central Park, adapted from similar English structures,

Treehouse on the Augustus Busch Estate in Michingan, 1911

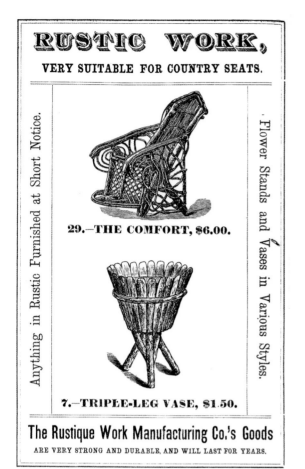

Page from 1881 catalog

were formative on the imagination and ambition of the industrialists and railroad barons who lived just across the street from Central Park on Fifth Avenue. He claims that these families, the Whitneys, Rockefellers, and Carnegies, actually brought the concept of rustic into the Adirondacks, where it found a rich new home, plenty of materials, space, and a labor pool of inventive craftsmen. They literally imported this rustic park idiom into the Adirondacks!

Suburban housing as we know it today developed after 1900 and accelerated quickly, thanks to the automobile, the highway system, and modular, low-cost housing materials. With this came the trend of furnishing and decorating porches, yards, and gardens. The oldest rustic furniture company in America, Old Hickory Furniture, started in 1899 in Shelbyville, Indiana. The catalog the company launched in 1902 marks the

Stereoscopic photographs of Central Park, late 19th century

Roadside stand, North Carolina

start of the mass appeal of rustic and reveals quite a bit about the tastes of the day.

One other historical influence on rustic in America was the huge migration from the British Isles in the 1820s through the turn of the 20th century. The Irish, English, Welsh, and Scottish farmers brought with them country woodcraft skills that were easily adapted to the woods and thickets of the Eastern seaboard and Appalachia, where many of them settled. It's likely that much of what we consider Appalachian rustic work, the twiggy-based tables and the bent chairs, have their design roots in the Irish and English countryside with their generations of bodgers and coppice workers.

There are other, smaller, feeder streams of rustic inspirations. Elements of Native American culture—the long house, the wigwam, the wickiup, the use of bark and bent forms— were adapted into the grammar of rustic.

Debris Hut at The Wilderness School, Brunswick, ME. Photo by Daniel Mack

Driftwood folly, Block Island, RI. Photo by Daniel Mack

Although Indians made some of the furniture for tourists and city shops, this style was never a central part of their domestic life. Today, there are still pockets of ethnic families in Florida, Appalachia, and Pennsylvania making quick, cheap outdoor furniture from white cedar scraps, willow, and cypress. These "gypsy" builders have been an uninterrupted source of American leisure furniture since early in the 20th century.

So those of us who head to the backyard are stepping into a long and rich tradition of adventurous makers. In the last quarter century, rustic has come to mean more than furniture or garden structures. It signals a receptivity toward living with surprise, as well as the practice of playful ingenuity—the pleasure of making creative use of a stick, a tree, a stone, a leaf, a piece of bark, driftwood—and seeing what happens. The measure of good rustic, today as in the past, is the delight it brings not only to the makers but also to those who buy a twig chair or a driftwood table and bring it home to live with and cherish.

Driftwood beach pavilion erected by Susan Churchill. Photo by William Gilmore

BUILDING WITH STICKS

Getting Ready to Build

If you're new to rustic work, you'll probably begin with a particular project in mind, and you'll find plenty of suitable starting points in the pages of this book. As you become more accustomed to building with limbs and vines, you may find that the materials at hand begin to suggest the forms they might take. Even when you stick strictly to the directions for a project, the look and feel of your chair or hat rack will be affected by the stock you gather. It's been said that sometimes you choose your pets, and sometimes your pets choose you. You'll find the same is true of the materials for rustic work. As you continue to build, you'll inevitably accumulate pieces of wood that strike you, and that you'll drag home because "someday I'll figure out what to do with it." In any case, we're not in the lumberyard anymore, Toto.

Gathering and Choosing Materials

Where should I look, and when? Start looking for materials whenever you're out of the house. You might find suitable stuff, especially for small projects, right in your own yard or just down the block. Keep an eye out for neighbors trimming their trees and bushes or for utility companies, park maintenance workers, or tree trimmers cutting in your area. You may have to work quickly, since most trimmings get fed to the chipper as soon as they're cut.

Maybe you have wooded areas close to where you live. You can undertake your initial reconnaissance mission from your car, especially if you get off the main highways and explore like-ly looking back roads. You'll begin to get a feel for the variety of woody plants that grow in your area. Keep a record of where you see lots of vines or willows or other species you might use in the future. Then get out of the car, and poke around. This way you'll know what tools you'll need to bring (see Gathering Tools, page 23) and which paths will be most productive. Be sure to ask landowners for permission before entering private land or beginning any bush-whacking.

You can gather materials for your rustic proj-ects at any time of the year, although your intentions for a particular piece may limit your schedule. For instance, a tightly woven form will be easier with new willow shoots gathered and used in the late spring. If you're planning a sturdy, durable chair, the saplings or branches may be gathered any time of the year, but you'll need to wait some time for them to dry. The rule of thumb is one year of air drying for each inch of diameter.

Many factors affect how fast wood dries. Softer woods tend to dry more quickly. Pieces with their bark left on dry more slowly. Since moisture travels more freely lengthwise in a stem, short pieces dry substantially more quick-ly than long pieces of the same diameter. Dry your stock, loosely stacked, off the ground in a dry location that provides both cover and free air circulation. If you have to dry your wood indoors, use open windows and a fan when you

can to speed the drying process. Whether you dry your stock indoors or out, check frequently for signs of insect infestations: new holes in the wood and piles of sawdust.

If you plan to peel the bark from the material you gather, you're best off harvesting in the early spring, when the rising sap and vigorous growth render bark looser. Peel the bark as soon as you can after cutting your stock, using a short-bladed knife to start lifting the bark. Avoid cutting into the new wood just inside the cambium layer, from which wood grows on the inside and bark grows on the outside. See Bark, on page 43, and Gathering and Weaving Hickory Bark, on page 81, for more appealing information.

While the specifics of proper drying and sea-sonal harvesting are important, don't let them dishearten you. If this is your first rustic project, and you want to get started, use whatever wood you can gather, and go to it. You may not wind up with a piece that will last for generations, and you may have to reinforce a joint later with screws or dowels, but you'll be able to enjoy the

Brian Creelman peeling a log

Start peeling with a short knife.

experience of making and using your project now. Immediacy is one of the great joys of rustic work—you might as well start creating pieces and start building up your rustic stockpile at the same time.

Rustic Joinery

Rustic work involves relatively few joining techniques—the fun comes with inventing ways of employing them. Let's talk about the basic ways of connecting the pieces before we decide what tools will be useful.

Here's a complete list of rustic joining methods:
- Gluing
- Binding
- Weaving
- Mechanical fastening
- Mortise and tenon

It's not a very intimidating list, is it? Understanding the strengths and weaknesses of these different techniques will allow you to choose the most appropriate joints for your creations.

GLUING

Small sticks can simply be glued together if the joint will not be stressed. Terry Taylor's Twig Letters (page 28) are a perfect example of a project where gluing will suffice. The surfaces to be glued should fit together without gaps so that the glue can hold them. The closer two sticks get to lying parallel with each other, the stronger a glue joint between them will be. Long-grain surfaces glue better than short-grain ones. (This means that you shouldn't expect sticks glued end-to-end to remain stuck for very long.)

For simple unstressed joints in projects intended for well-protected areas, white craft glue works fine. Such glue joints won't work well for pieces used outdoors because the wood will expand and contract both seasonally and between wet and dry days. However, structural epoxy intended for marine use will hold well-crafted glue joints, especially if appropriate thickening agents have been added. (Check the manufacturer's specifications for proper applications.) Remember with all types of glue: the drier the wood the better the glue joint.

Glue also reinforces mortise and tenon joints. Woodworking glues formulated for exterior use hold well in relatively tight joints, but they won't fill gaps with much strength. Structural epoxy, while more expensive, can help sloppier joints. Use additives such as microfibers or colloidal silica, available where you buy the glue, to thicken epoxy so that it stays where you put it.

BINDING

Use wire or twine to hold elements of your construction in place temporarily while you consider their effect or plan the joinery. Any kind of wire works for this as long as it's strong enough for the job. Take several turns around the sticks, and tighten the ends with a few twists.

For more permanent bound joints, use bare or sheathed copper, galvanized steel, or stainless steel wire. Your choice will depend on appearance, unless the binding is going to be concealed with vines or bark strips. Marcia Whitt's Flower Tower (page 32) uses this technique.

Bound fencing

Vines and hickory strips can be used for natural binding materials. Such connections remain quite sturdy since you wrap the vines or strips while they're green. The binding shrinks and hardens as it dries, pulling the bound elements together.

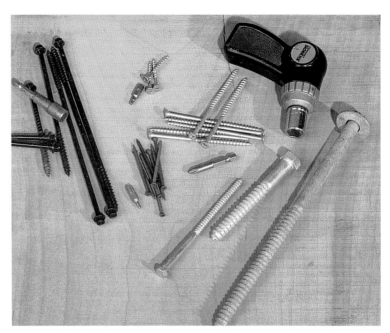

TimberLok, drywall, coated, and lag screws; hex, square, and Philips driver inserts, hand ratchet driver

Beginning a twisted-pair weave

WEAVING

Several projects in this book employ weaving as their primary structural joint, and several others derive some of their strength from woven elements. Of course, weaving can also add considerable visual strength to a rustic composition.

As you know, weaving simply means lacing one set of flexible elements alternately in front of and behind another set of elements running at right angles to the first set. The tighter the weave, the stronger the joint. As with binding with vines, you'll weave using green wood that will harden as it dries, "setting" its curves. This can produce a sturdy structure if the vines or withes are pushed tight enough that their elasticity keeps forcing the pieces together as they dry. A very loose weave can become looser as it shrinks and hardens. In this case, you might reinforce some of the crossings with small nails.

MECHANICAL FASTENINGS

While nails and screws might seem "unrustic," many rustic pieces would be much harder to make without them. You can use these fasteners to make secure, long-lasting connections by themselves or to reinforce other kinds of joints. Nails can even present a decorative opportunity if you choose copper or rose-head fasteners. Be aware that some copper nails you'll find in the hardware store are merely copper-plated steel. Hitting these with a hammer will chip the coating, exposing the steel to moisture and leading to rust—a little too rustic an effect. Look for copper or bronze nails in marine supply stores or online, or check the source list at the Lark Books Web site (www.larkbooks.com).

Use metal fasteners manufactured for exterior or marine use: galvanized or epoxy-coated decking screws, galvanized finish nails, copper nails, bronze or stainless steel screws, and, for larger projects, galvanized lag screws, barn spikes, and threaded rod. Dan Mack highly recommends TimberLok screws for their superior strength, holding ability, and hexagonal heads.

MORTISE AND TENON JOINTS

While cabinetmakers have devised dozens of varieties of mortise and tenon joints, the kinds of mortise and tenon joints used in rustic work can be counted on one and a half fingers. We

End Blocks for Accurate Joinery

Brian Creelman uses a versatile method for boring accurately angled mortises. He concentrates on the centerline of each element in a construction. Even if a particular branch is curved or twirled or wavy, he establishes a centerline and attaches appropriately sized squares of plywood to its ends so that the centers of the end blocks align with the centerline of the whole piece. This way, the ends of a stick don't necessarily have to coincide with the centerline of the stick. For instance, the bottom end of a chair leg can veer off to the side without unduly complicating the task of cutting accurate joints.

Here's how it works: Say you're making a post-and-rung chair. You would normally build the side panels (front post, back post, and two or three rungs, each), and then connect them with the front and back rungs. To use end blocks to help construct a side panel, cut four 3"- or 4"-squares from ½" plywood. Draw diagonals to find the center, and drive a 1⅝" drywall screw through the center of each square so that about ½" of the tip protrudes on the other side. Determine the centerlines of your front and back posts, and drive the screws into the ends of the posts at those lines, aligning one side of the square with what will be the side of the chair. (If the top ends of the posts will show, you can allow extra length there to be trimmed off later.) If a centerline falls outside the end of a post, align the screw with the centerline, and drive a second screw through the plywood and into the post. Now the two squares on each post should line up with each other, and the edges of the squares should hold the posts so that the side rung mortises can be drilled vertically. You also have a good surface to measure from to position the mortises. Furthermore, by rolling the posts and squares 90°, you can drill the front or back mortises vertically as well. That would produce a square chair seat.

You can make a refinement to the system to make it easy to bore mortises for chairs in which the seat is wider in the front. Determine the difference between the centerline width of the front posts and the back posts. It might be 3", or 1½" on each side. Cut the squares for the back post end blocks 3" larger than the squares for the front post. After the side has been assembled (notice that the end blocks help prevent twist in the panel), you can turn the end blocks so that they all have an edge flat against the table. Now the side panel of the chair has the proper angle to enable drilling vertical holes for the front and back rungs.

use a round tenon (or peg) in a round hole. Sometimes the tenon goes right through the mortise (the hole), and sometimes that tenon is wedged for a tighter fit, but the basic format is always the same.

For long-lasting mortise and tenon joints, you should always use dry wood. The stick that will have the mortise (hole) drilled into it can be greener than the stick with the tenon (peg) that goes into it, because as the greener stick dries, the mortise will shrink around the tenon, creating a firm joint. But remember: this won't work if that mortised stick also has a tenon on its end because the tenon will also shrink, creating a loose joint. That being said, we'll repeat: if you're new to rusticating and fired up to get going on a project, you can always use the wood you have on hand, even if it means reinforcing some joints with screws or dowels later on if things loosen up a bit.

Begin with the mortise. The size of the hole you bore will depend on the sizes of the two pieces you're joining. Generally, the hole's diameter equals one third to one half of the diameter of the piece it's bored in. Naturally, the hole can't be bigger than the tenoned stick, or there's no joint at all. If it's a blind mortise (one that doesn't go all the way through), the hole should extend as deep as is practical. That provides more surface for glue or the wood alone to grip, resulting in a stronger joint. Even the largest mortises need be no deeper than 3" or 4". In Building Tools (page 23), we'll talk about various ways of boring mortise holes.

By its very nature, rustic work involves sticks meeting each other at odd angles. This means with a mortise and tenon joint, you have two options: you can make the joint at a right angle to the mortised piece, shaping the tenon to that angle, or you can cut a tenon in line with its stick,

Beginning a large tenon

Rounding a tenon

and angle the mortise appropriately. In most instances, the latter method works best. In tricky panel constructions, where several tenons must go into one mortised piece at the same time, you might choose the first option.

To bore angled mortises, lay the pieces to be joined in their intended positions with the mortised piece on top. Mark the center of the mortise. You may need to raise the piece to be mortised in order to drill the hole. Prop it on some blocks, clamp it, or get a friend to hold it while you bore the hole, using the tenon piece as an angle guide. You can also use an adjustable

bevel to take the angle of the joint. Then you can move the mortise piece to a vise and use the adjustable bevel to guide your drilling.

In a blind mortise and tenon joint, the tenon should fit snugly into its mortise, without quite touching the back of the hole. "Snugly" means that you can twist and shove the tenon home, perhaps using a few mallet taps to drive the last little bit. Achieve this fit with hand tools like knives, chisels, round-soled spokeshaves, and rasps or files. Marking the length of the tenon (just short of the depth of the mortise) on the stick will give you a sense of where you should

Whittling a small tenon, using a sizing block, and compressed tenon fibers

start cutting the shoulder (the place where the size of the stick starts being reduced). Try to make a tight radius between the shoulder and the tenon. You can produce different looks with short or long transitions between the stick diameter and the tenon, but a very gradual one tends to look sloppy and reduces the strength of the joint. The joint should be stopped from closing farther by the shoulder area, not the bottom of the mortise. Chop, whittle, and rasp until your cylindrical tenon just fits into the mortise.

Wedged through tenons on an old bench seat

For sizing small tenons, use a piece of hardwood with a mortise-size hole drilled through it. Not only does this allow you to see where you still have to trim, pushing and twisting the tenon into the hole compresses its fibers, ensuring a tight fit. See the photos on the previous page of Daniel Mack using a sizing block.

Making a through mortise follows the same steps as a blind joint except that the hole goes all the way through the mortised piece, and the tenon must be correspondingly longer. Since most bits will tear out splinters and bark when they exit a limb, you should use an auger bit or a spade bit for boring a through mortise. Both tools have a long center point that breaks through before the main cutters, allowing you to stop, back the bit out, and complete the hole from the other side. Just use the center hole to position the bit.

The through tenon needs careful shaping because the fit will show on the other side. You can make the tenon just a little longer than the hole or let it stick out more dramatically, as Paul Ruhlmann does to good effect in his

Peeled-Pole Trellis and Obelisk (page 116), but never leave it short. That always looks like a mistake rather than an aesthetic statement.

You can strengthen your mortise and tenon joints with glue, with a nail, screw, or dowel driven through the thickness of the tenon, or with a wedge driven into the end of a through tenon. To use glue, put a little all the way around the inside of the mortise, just under the lip. The tenon pushes the glue along and spreads it inside the joint. Wipe off the excess

Wedged tenon parts ready to assemble

Driving the wedge

from the outside of a through joint and around the shoulder if any squeezes out around a blind joint.

To hold a tenon in place even if the joint loosens, you can drive a nail right through all parts of the joint. The nail should be just shorter than the thickness of the mortised piece. A dowel can be driven in the same way, but you must drill a hole for the dowel. Don't assume that the ¼" dowel you bought will really fill a ¼" hole. The next smaller drill size might work better. When using a screw, try drilling a hole the size of the outside diameter of the screw threads, but only slightly into the tenon. When you drive the screw, there's a good chance the tenon will split and fill the mortise more tightly.

Using a wooden wedge to strengthen a through tenon produces the same effect as a screw. The difference is that you choose the placement of the split by sawing a kerf down the length of the tenon before it's placed through its mortise. Any handsaw works well for this. The kerf should run across the grain of the mortised stick, so the wedge pushes the

tenon parts against the end grain, thereby avoiding splitting the mortised piece. The most difficult part of making this joint is making a wedge that fits. The wedge should fill the kerf and all gaps in the joint (plus a little more) before it hits the bottom of the kerf. You can whittle wedges from hardwood, or you might try using shims from the home improvement store, but they are generally softwood and have a tendency to split. Push the joint together, squeeze a little glue into the saw kerf, and drive the wedge until it's tight. Trim the end of the tenon with a small handsaw. A Japanese saw works especially well here. See Andy Rae's Slab Desk project for an application of this joint (page 52).

Tenon Cutters

I've waited until now to talk about tenon cutters because I didn't want to scare you into thinking that you absolutely need one to make rustic mortise and tenon joints. Tenon cutters use a small blade to form a particular diameter tenon and a radiused shoulder. If kept sharp they work well, especially when chucked in a power drill. You can also drive them with a brace, but get ready for a slow ride. Tenon cutters can be

Veritas Tenon Cutter and its product

The basic rustic gathering kit: leather gloves, tie-down strap, folding saw, pruning shears, bungee cord

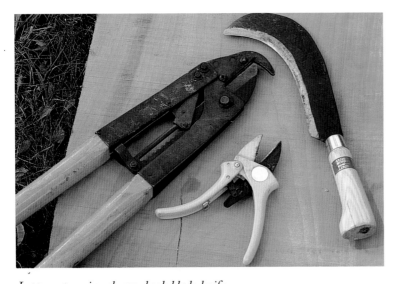

Loppers, pruning shears, hook blade knife

Small bucksaw, panel saw, folding saws

"exciting" to use, and they are not cheap. In addition, each cutter forms one diameter tenon, so you might need several for one chair, for instance. Try shaping some tenons by hand to get the hang of that process first, and you'll soon find out whether you need tenon cutters and, if you do, what sizes to get. I should add that every serious rustic maker now uses tenon cutters all the time. They save considerable time and improve accuracy. The Veritas Tenon Cutter available from Lee Valley Tools has become the quality standard.

Useful Tools

Let's keep it simple. You don't need all the tools in the following list, at least not right away. Choose the ones you need for the projects you want to make, and buy more as you need them. Purchase the best tools you can—there's a big difference in quality between cheap and expensive, bigger than the cost difference. A good tool makes the job easier and more pleasurable. Shop flea markets for good old tools that need only cleaning and sharpening. Concentrate on hand tools to begin with. Sure, a chain saw can cut a lot of wood in a hurry, but a sharp bucksaw can too, with less cost, less noise, less air pollution, and less to carry into the woods. You'll know when you need the chain saw. One more piece of wisdom about power tools: you'll

Battery-powered reciprocating saw and mini chain saw

make your mistakes more slowly with hand tools, often stopping in time to avert tragedy. That goes for body parts as well as pieces of wood. With those caveats, let's dig into the tool chest.

GATHERING TOOLS

Note that you can carry all of these in a backpack. Daniel Mack often goes into the woods with only gloves, a small pruning saw, pruning shears, and a couple of bungee cords.

Gloves. Be sure to have good hand protection against thorns and other rough edges. Leather is more flexible than canvas.

Tape measure. If you know what you're looking for, you can save a lot of backache by cutting to likely lengths where you find the material. (On the other hand, it's fun to have plenty of interesting stuff to choose from as your project evolves.)

Pruning shears. For cutting stems and branches up to ½" in diameter. Look for one-handed shears with straight or curved blades.

Loppers. Long handles provide more leverage for cutting through branches and saplings up to 1½" in diameter. Models with gears or ratchets require less muscle power.

Pruning saw. For bigger branches, saplings, and the occasional trunk, a pruning saw is indispensable. A narrow blade with Japanese-style, diamond-shaped teeth cuts fast on the pull stroke, and the best ones fold into the handle to stow safely in your toolbag or a deep pocket.

Bow saw or bucksaw. For taking down small trees and big branches, look for models with 16" to 24" blades, which have enough stroke length to let you cut through the big stuff. Get a blade guard or buy a folding or knock-down model for easy packing into the woods.

Hook blade lopping knife. For quickly clearing small branches and suckers from a log.

Rope, bungee cord, or nylon tie-down straps. For bundling and toting your new stash back to the road.

Hatchets and adzes

BUILDING TOOLS

Lumber crayon, carpenter's pencil. For making broad marks that are easy to see on rough or dark surfaces.

Penknife. For whittling, carving, and trimming small tenons.

Crosscut saw. For cutting parts to length. A short, 10-teeth-per-inch saw works well for all but the largest limbs.

Drawknife, hatchet, drawknife with folding handles

Double-twist, brad point, spade, Forstner, single-spur, and multi-tooth bits

Battery-driven sawzall or chain saw. While not very powerful, these can come in handy for cutting small logs to length.

Japanese ryoba and dozuki saws. For cutting to length and trimming joints and branches. Japanese saws cut on the pull stroke instead of on the push stoke, as Western saws do. They're easier to control because they require less force, and the thin blade tracks more accurately. The ryoba corresponds to a carpenter's saw, except that it has two sawing edges, one for ripping with the grain and one for crosscutting

Cordless drill with hole saws

against the grain. A dozuki has a sturdy back, so its blade can be even thinner and more flexible. Dozukis use closely set, fine teeth to make smooth cuts. They can cut flush with an adjoining surface and reach into tight spots. Many dozukis have replaceable blades, a good thing because you wouldn't want to sharpen all those tiny teeth. Because of the thin kerf they make, Japanese saws tend to bind in all but dry, docile timber. They still work beautifully for trimming the ends of tenons or legs.

Hatchet. For trimming twigs from branches and for splitting limbs into halves, quarters, or slats. With a mallet to apply force, you can use the hatchet as a controlled splitting wedge.

Claw hammer, tack hammer. For driving everything from brads to spikes, and for making those subtle "adjustments" during assembly.

Chisels and a mallet. For cutting tenons and carving. Chisel widths between ¼" and 1½" will find the most use. Remember to keep chisels sharp, and secure your workpiece with clamps or a vise.

Vise, clamps, string, and twine. For holding your work temporarily.

Spokeshave, drawknife. For controlled or aggressive shaping. The spokeshave works like a very short plane, taking a shaving of wood at a time. You can push it or pull it to produce a smooth surface or to shape a tenon. As its name implies, you pull a drawknife toward you to remove material with its open blade. With the bevel down, control the depth of cut by changing the angle of the handles. A drawknife can remove stubborn bark easily, leaving a tooled surface.

Brace and double-twist auger bits. For quickly and quietly boring holes. I often prefer a brace and bit to a spade bit or Forstner bit in an electric drill, even when working with kiln-dried hardwoods. If you've only tried an auger with a dull, single-twist bit, you don't know how easily a brace and bit can cut. Double-twist bits cut more efficiently. You do have to keep your bits sharp, so get a little file made for this purpose. With the brace and the lead screw on auger bits, it's easy to drill a hole through a branch without chipping out the other side. When you're nearly through, the screw center will emerge from the other side. Stop there, back the auger out, and drill from the other side using the screw hole as your guide.

Cordless drill. Models with ⅜" chucks and 12- to 18-volt batteries have the capacity to drill big holes in thick stock. Keep a charged, spare battery on hand.

Electric drill. For driving tenon cutters, especially the larger sizes where a ½" capacity and an auxiliary handle are necessary.

Driver bits. For driving screws with a power drill. They're available in Phillips, straight, and square-drive styles, and as sockets for driving TimberLok screws or lag screws.

Brad-point bits. For drilling holes up to ½" diameter.

Spade bits. For drilling deep holes and large-diameter mortises These inexpensive bits work well if they're kept sharp, which you can do easily with a grinder. You can also grind the sides of the bit to make tapered holes and to size the bit for a particular tenon cutter.

Forstner bits. Much more expensive than spade bits, their advantage comes in drilling flat-bottom holes without a lead screw. Because they're partially rim-guided, it's sometimes hard to get them started in the intended spot. Use a drill press to eliminate this problem. Forstner bits tend to clog in sizes smaller than ¾".

Hole saws. For cutting short tenons. You'll have to find (or grind to size) a spade bit that matches the inside diameter of the saw, but hole saws make effective and inexpensive tenon cutters. Trim off the excess wood at the shoulder with a saw or gouge or knife.

Tenon cutters. Varieties of dowel and tenon cutters have been around for a long time, so you might find one for your brace at the flea market. An excellent new tenon cutter, co-designed by one of our contributing designers, Paul Ruhlmann, and available from Lee Valley

Hand- and drill-driven dowel cutters

Tools, produces a smooth tenon with a tightly radiused shoulder. It's an aggressive cutter, so secure your stock in a vise, and hold the drill firmly as you advance the cutter. A ½" heavy-duty drill with a side handle is required for the larger sizes (1¼" to 3"). These cutters work so well that, if you're doing any amount of rustic building, they're well worth the investment.

Chop saw, drill press. These two stationery tools can increase your efficiency and your safety. Round stock like saplings and branches cannot be handled safely on many power tools. Because of the built-in v-block formed by the

Veritas Tenon Cutters with ½" electric drill for cutting large tenons and cordless drill for cutting small ones

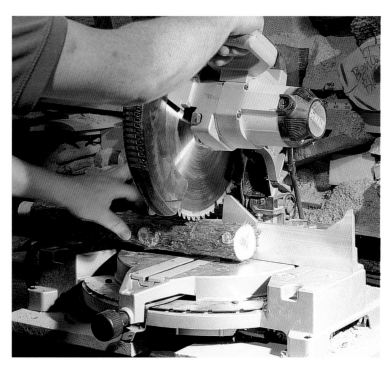

Chop saw, using table and fence as v-block

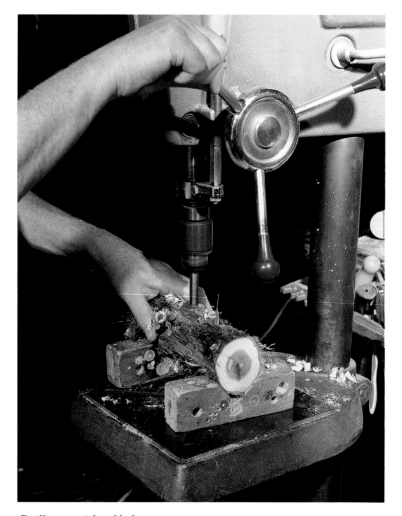

Drill press with v-blocks

chop saw's table and fence, branches can easily be held in place and kept from rolling. The drill press easily and accurately bores even large diameter holes once you've made v-blocks to help hold the stock. Be ready to use clamps when you need additional help.

Finishing

Rustic work requires very little care and feeding in the finish department. Bark-on pieces don't need any finish—they bring their own. Some makers sand exposed ends and brush on yellow shellac, which inhibits moisture transfer somewhat and presents a more finished appearance. You can use a penetrating oil finish on peeled wood, but its natural surface shines nicely, too.

No finish can keep out rot spores and the moisture they need to grow, and rot is the major enemy of outdoor furniture. Keeping your pieces out of direct contact with the ground will help preserve them. Don't let them sit in puddles on decks or patios, either. To preserve your work that must stand on soil, raise it slightly—use plastic pipe for small pieces and concrete for larger ones. For a chair or table that need not move often, drive 6" to 8" lengths of 1" plastic pipe into the ground directly under the legs, leaving a just a little above the surface. Whittle the ends of the legs to fit into the pipes. Now you have an unobtrusive platform that you can still mow over.

The ends of legs can also be protected with a thick coat of structural epoxy, which can prevent moisture transfer. Thicken the epoxy with manufacturer-recommended additives to a honey consistency to keep it in place until it cures. It helps to prop up the piece so that the leg bottoms are level. In any case, watch for dribbles during the first hour or two, and wipe them off with paper towels or a flexible putty knife.

The Projects

We invited talented rustic makers from the United States and Canada to contribute projects for you to build. The rustic world today encompasses a great variety of makers and styles. Some of these artists have been using rustic materials for many years, while others are relatively new converts. Women are as likely as men to carve out at least part of their living by making and installing rustic work, and the work itself ranges from delicate willow weaving to strenuous vine constructions. Use these projects as recipes to follow or merely as points of departure—they're intended to inspire your imagination and to suggest appropriate techniques. As you read the projects and create your versions of them, send a thought of thanks for the generosity of the designers in sharing them with us.

There are 30 projects in all, organized into four sections—Fun & Fast, Porch & Deck, Seating: Outdoors or Indoors, and Garden & Yard. They range in difficulty from delightfully easy to remarkably challenging.

In all cases we have tried to make the project instructions as clear as possible, but the nature of rustic materials sometimes leads to confusing terminology and lack of specificity in dimensions. Let's try to clear the fog a little.

First, in the Materials lists, we often provide specific dimensions, but you should understand them to say "about." We don't always have the branches we want to use in the sizes listed, so we come close, and adjust the dimensions of other pieces if we need to. All dimensions listed are approximate, and you should work accordingly. A general rule in woodworking is even more appropriate to rustic work: Don't cut until you have to. Its corollary applies as well: Measure directly, by holding the new piece up to what is already in place.

Second, the names we use for the pieces of trees included in the projects are advisory only. If the instructions say "sapling," and you have a branch, go ahead and use it. By looking at the photos and the drawings, and by using your imagination, you can tell if the crooked stick in your hand will make a chair leg or not. Rustic building depends upon, and exults in, flexibility. Go with the gnarly flow, and use what you have.

TWIG LETTERS

Designed by Terry Taylor

These letters make nice decorations outdoors or inside. Daniel Mack talks about finding the chair in the tree. Here's a simple project that encourages you to see entire poems in the forest.

MATERIALS

Twigs

SUPPLIES & TOOLS

Wire or twist-ties

Needles or pins

White craft glue or woodworking glue

150-grit sandpaper

Fine saw

Sharp nippers

Knife

Drill and bits

Pliers

Forming the Letters

1 There are many ways to fashion letters and numbers from twigs. Several are illustrated in figure 1. Let's start at the end.

2 The "Y" is simply a forked twig cut to suit. "I," "L," "V," "l," "r," "v," and "y" could be made in the same way.

3 Tie a forked twig and a straight one with wire or a twist-tie to make the "k."

4 This small "i" consists of a straight twig and a short section of a larger twig held apart with a wire. You can use a short needle or a straight pin with the head nipped off. Use the pliers to push the needle into the dot first. It will slide into the end of the small twig more easily.

5 Make the sharp corners of the "w" with miter joints. Nip your twig into approximate lengths, then arrange them to form the letter. Where they cross, use a fine saw to bisect the crossing, so that the sawn ends are similarly shaped. You may need to adjust the ends by rubbing them on a sheet of sandpaper laid flat on your work surface. Once all the joints have been cut and adjusted, glue them together one by one, holding them until the glue begins to set up. You can reinforce these joints with small straight pins.

6 The "t" has tiny versions of classic rustic mortise and tenon joints. Choose a drill bit slightly smaller than the twigs for the horizontal arms. Drill straight through the vertical twig. Whittle the ends of the crossing twigs until they just push into the hole. Press them in tightly, and you probably won't need any glue.

7 Letters and numbers with curved lines can be made with fresh twigs flexible enough to form the shape required. Tie closed shapes like the circle of a "b" with fine wire. For a neater job, cut scarf joints—matching angled surfaces as shown in figure 1—and wrap them with wire. You can make open curved lines by using string or wire to hold the desired shape of green twigs until they dry and keep the imposed shape. Over-bend the curves to allow for a little spring back.

8 Small letters like these can stand on their own or be glued to wooden bases.

9 The techniques used for small letters will also work for larger figures. Only the sizes of the joints and the force required to bend the sticks change. You can even use bundles of vines or willow shoots wired together to form both straight and curved lines.

Figure 1

LOG CANDLEHOLDERS

Designed by Tammy M. Perrine

*T*hese simple and quick-to-make candleholders will provide a romantic atmosphere for your patio. Local varieties of thick vines will work as well as small logs.

MATERIALS

Bases: limbs, various sizes

SUPPLIES & TOOLS

Candle inserts

Handsaw

Plane

Vise or clamp

Drill press or electric drill with spade bits

Small rubber mallet or hammer

Sandpaper

Yellow shellac or oil finish

Making the Candleholders

1 Find suitable limbs for the bases. The photograph shows some straightforward bases, but you might want to explore more gnarly terrain. Pay attention to stability—you don't want your lit candles falling over. The vertical bases should not be too high, and horizontal bases may need planing.

2 The candle inserts come in ⅝" and ⅞" sizes. Drill some test holes to find the correct bit. The insert should require some force to seat it fully. With the larger insert, you might start with a 1" spade bit. You may have to grind away a portion from each side of the bit to achieve a good fit. Use a vise or a clamp to hold your base securely while boring. For a more finished appearance on the horizontal base, Tammy Perrine used a larger bit first to provide a flat area for the lip of the candle insert. Seat the inserts with a small rubber mallet or a cloth-covered hammer.

3 Sand the end grain of the base, beginning with 60- or 80-grit paper, and work your way up to 220 grit. If you wish, finish the end grain with yellow shellac or an oil finish.

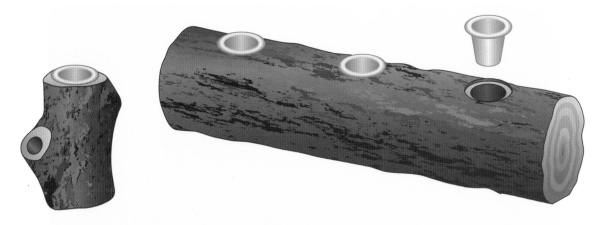

Figure 1

FLOWER TOWER

Designed by Marcia Whitt

Here's a pretty freestanding trellis for your vines that is remarkably sturdy, thanks to its tipi design and woven sides. Place it anywhere in your garden, and let morning glories, ivy, red runner beans, or sweet peas climb toward the sun.

MATERIALS

Poles: 7 straight willow sticks, at least 7' long

Temporary platform: 1¼" plywood circle, 21" diameter

Weavers: slender willow branches

SUPPLIES & TOOLS

Nails, assorted sizes

Wire for temporary binding

Boiled linseed oil and mineral spirits (optional, see step 8)

Hammer

Pliers or wire cutters

Pruning shears

Building the Tipi

1 Mark seven evenly spaced positions around the edge of the plywood circle. Put the circle on the ground, and go find a friend. Have him or her hold the long poles above the plywood circle in a loose bundle near their thinner ends, while you move the lower ends out to your marks to form a tipi. Nail the bottom ends to the edge of the plywood disc at their marked positions, leaving the nail heads proud to make removing the nails easier.

2 Bind the posts tightly near their tops with the wire. Nail the posts to their neighbors where they cross (hold a heavy object against

the posts while nailing to make the task easier). Remove the wire.

Weaving the Willow Bands

3 Mark each stick at 16" and 24" from the ground. The lower band of weaving will fill the space between these marks. Sort your willow by thickness into three piles. The thickest willows will be used in the bottom band of weaving, those that are a little thicker will be woven in the middle band, and the thinnest willow will be used for winding at the top of the tower.

4 Begin with the thickest willow. Start at the bottom marks on the poles and nail the thick end of one weaver to the inside of a post. Begin weaving in and out around the posts. (You may have to bend the thick end of the willow back and forth in your hands to make it pliable enough to weave.) The end of the weaver should stop behind a post. Start a new weaver (thick-end-first) behind the post where the previous thin end stops. Nail the weavers to the insides of the posts to secure them at every thick end and elsewhere as necessary. Figure 1 on page 32 shows clearly the spacing of the three bands of weaving.

5 Continue weaving to the upper marks, keeping your rows tight and level, and nailing occasionally to keep them that way.

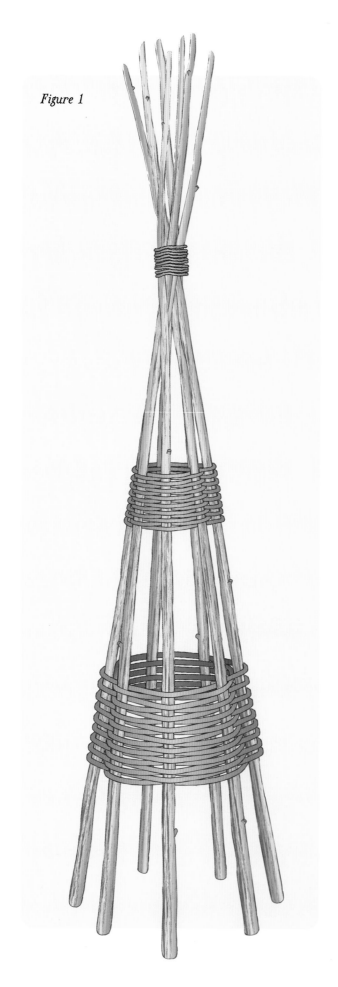

Figure 1

When you get to the last weaver, nail it to every post.

6 Decide where to put the middle band of the tower, about halfway up the open space above the first band. Measure from the ground, and mark each post for the bottom and top of the new band. This band should be narrower than the first. Weave as before, but with narrower willows to suit the tighter post spacing. Nail the weavers occasionally and all the way around the top weaver.

7 Use small, flexible willows to wrap tightly the area where the posts are nailed together. Tuck the ends between posts, and nail the windings to the posts to secure them.

Finishing the Tower

8 Remove the tower from the plywood disc by pulling the nails or by tapping the insides of the posts to loosen them. If you want to apply a finish to your tower, now is the time. Marcia Whitt recommends a mixture of one part boiled linseed oil and two parts mineral spirits to achieve a rich brown color. You can brush the finish or try a bottle sprayer.

9 When you decide where to place your tower, consider putting a stone or brick under each post to allow water to drain away from the wood. In a windy spot, you can secure the posts to stakes or short lengths of rebar driven into the ground. Use galvanized wire with the rebar and nails with wooden stakes.

LOG WALK

Designed by Daniel Mack

Here's a great way to keep your feet dry as you tour your yard or garden.

MATERIALS
Log

SUPPLIES & TOOLS
Chain saw or bucksaw

Making the Walk

1 Find a log.

2 Cut it into 2"-thick sections.

3 Arrange the sections on the ground.

4 Fill in with bark mulch.

Okay, it's not quite that simple. Nor does your walk have to look like Daniel's. You would do well to cut the slabs where you find the log rather than trying to drag it home. Better yet, contact a tree removal service, and ask them to cut sections for you.

Consider other arrangements as well. You could place sections closer together in a zigzag pattern to make a wider walkway or use smaller pieces to make a mosaic walk. Remember that the more pieces you use, the more ground preparation you may need to produce a smooth path.

RUSTIC RACK

Designed by Andy Rae

*T*he interplay between the rough and smooth wood turns this relatively simple rack into a playful piece for a porch or even a front hall. It's the perfect project for that gnarly or vine-wrapped limb you've been saving.

MATERIALS

Beam: 1 gnarly limb, 2" diameter x 40"

Posts: 1 limb, 2" diameter, long enough for two 15" pieces

Stretcher: 1 peeled stick, 1" diameter x 34"

Pegs: 6 peeled straight or forked twigs, 4" to 5" long

SUPPLIES & TOOLS

Woodworker's glue

2½" screws

Shellac

Trimming saw

Sharp knife

Coping saw

Chisel

Drill with ¼" or ½", and ⅜" bits

Building the Frame

1   With any luck, the limb you choose for the beam will have enough length to yield two posts, as well. With the front side up, cut the ends of the beam at an angle so that the end grain shows. Cut the posts to length in similar fashion.

2   The beam rides in notches in the posts, and the posts hold the stretcher in mortises. Mark out these joints as follows: Lay the beam and the stretcher stick on top of the posts, and arrange them in a pleasing composition. With a soft pencil or marker, reach under the stretcher to mark its centerline on the inside of each of the posts. Mark the ends of the stretcher about 1" past the inside edges of the posts. Angle the pencil to trace the upper and lower edges of the beam slightly inside its actual dimension.

3   Bore mortises in the posts for the stretcher at your centerline marks. These holes should be a little smaller than the diameter of the smaller end of the stretcher. Lay the stretcher a few inches from the holes to give yourself an indication of the proper angle for the holes. Drill about 1⅛" deep. Now cut the stretcher to length.

4   Use a sharp knife to whittle the stretcher ends into tenons to fit the mortises. Try to keep these tenons cylindrical, not tapered.

5   With the beam close by for reference, use a coping saw to cut a rounded notch, at your traced marks, about halfway through each post. If the outside (top and bottom) edges of the notch fit tightly against the back of the beam, you're finished.

Otherwise, deepen the notch with a chisel or knife.

6   Assemble the frame by putting woodworker's glue in each mortise and pushing the posts onto the ends of the stretcher. Put the beam in place, and hold the joints tightly while you turn the frame over. Drive one or two screws through the back of each notched joint.

Adding the Pegs and the Finish

7   Choose twigs for the pegs, and trim them, allowing for a 1" tenon. The pegs should be sturdy enough to hold garden tools, so don't make them too long or skinny.

8   Arrange the pegs along the beam, mark for the mortises, and bore holes 1⅛" deep at suitable angles for each peg. Whittle tenons on the pegs, put a little glue in the mortises, and push the pegs home.

9   You will want to sand or trim the top edges of the peg ends, at least. Do the same for the other exposed ends for a more finished look, and shellac the end grain if you wish. Hang your rack with short loops of leather or twine on common nails or screws, as shown.

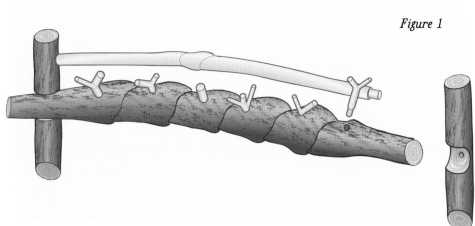

Figure 1

WOVEN PLANT SURROUND

Designed by Kim Vergil

*H*elp your peonies, Shasta daisies, and phlox stand proud with this easy project, which will give you the chance to weave freshly cut garden trimmings around your favorite plants.

MATERIALS

Stakes: an uneven number of sticks, length should match mature plant height

Weavers: willow branches (or other pliable plant trimmings), at least 40" long

SUPPLIES & TOOLS

Loppers

Pruning shears

Making the Surround

1 Gather your plant material. You'll need an uneven number of straight, dry sticks, enough to surround the base of the mature plant at intervals of about 3". The willow should be ⅛" to ½" in diameter and at least 40" long. You might find that your own garden trimmings from other plants are suitable for weaving.

2 Use loppers to cut a sharp point on the thick end of each stick.

3 Push the sticks 4" to 6" into the ground, distributing them evenly around the plant, about 3" apart. Flare the sticks outward a bit.

4 Select two weavers, and start the weaving 7" or 8" below the tops of the sticks. Begin with the fat ends of the weavers. Always work with two weavers at once. The idea is to twist the weavers together while weaving. Begin by holding the end of the first weaver against the outside of a stick, weaving it behind the next stick to the right and in front of the third stick.

5 Insert the end of the second weaver below the first weaver and behind the first stick. Bring the second weaver in front of the second stick, then above the first weaver to go behind the third stick and in front of the fourth. This weaver started below the first one and finished

on top. Repeat this twisting process throughout the weaving.

6 Pick up the first weaver, bringing it over and behind the next stick and in front of the fifth. Continue to weave in turn each lagging weaver in this manner all the way around the circle. Twisting and weaving like this produces a sturdy structure.

7 When you're finished with the first pair, tuck it inside the structure. Begin a new pair five sticks to the left or right of the first stick, depending on whether your weavers are longer or shorter than the circumference of your circle. This ensures that the weavers don't all start at the same place. Weave and twist the next pair as you did the first, keeping it tight against the previous weaving. Weave around the circle until you have a 3" band.

8 Finally, trim the sticks a few inches above the weaving.

BIRCH BARK WINDOW BOX

Designed by Cheryl Evans

Here's a project where the hard work has been done—you get to do the fun part. Start with a purchased cedar window box. Add birch bark, a simple trellis, and classic twig-work trim, and you have a charming window box that would also make a cozy home for indoor potted plants.

MATERIALS

Trellis uprights: 7 willow saplings,
½" diameter x 18"

Trellis weaving: 4 to 8 willow saplings,
¼" to ⅜" diameter x 30"

Twig work: at least 30 alder, willow, or
red osier twigs, ¼" to ½" diameter,
various lengths

Cedar window box

White birch bark

SUPPLIES & TOOLS

Contact cement

1" brown or black paneling nails

Exterior polyurethane spray

Loppers

Garden pruners

Strong scissors or utility knife

Ruler

Brayer (optional)

Hammer

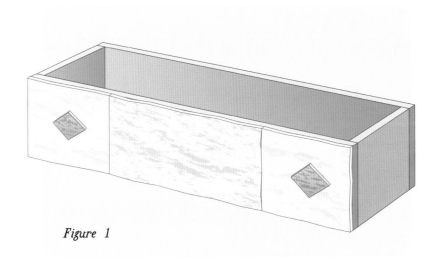

Figure 1

Covering the Box with Bark

1 You can gather your own bark from fallen birch trees or buy it from craft stores or catalogs. The golden brown accent diamonds come from the underlying layers of white birch bark. Choose your bark for the panels on the front and sides, as shown in figure 3 on page 42. You can cover the back, too, if you wish. Try for a balanced look. Mark the front to divide it into three sections, with the middle one larger than the other two.

2 Using the marked front sections as guides, cut the bark for these three sections with heavy scissors or a utility knife and a ruler (cut a little large at first, then trim to size). Follow the same procedure to cut the end panels. Apply contact cement to the box and the bark, following the manufacturer's instructions. Press the bark firmly in place, remembering you have only one chance to position it. Push it down

hard, everywhere, using a brayer if you have one.

3 Peel off the outer layers of another piece of bark until you find a color that contrasts with the rest of the bark. Cut your diamond-shaped pieces from this, and glue them to the front of the box, centered in the outer front panels (see figure 1).

Adding the Trellis

4 Now we'll add the trellis, which is nailed to the inside of the box. You can use forked sticks for some of the uprights to add interest. Decide on an angle for the end uprights, and trace those two sticks on the inside of the box. (See figure 2 for a sample arrangement.) Because it will be difficult to hammer inside the box, before putting each stick in position, hammer its first nail partway into the wood near the end of the stick. Then place the stick in position and complete the fastening with the side of your hammer. Add another nail near the top edge of the box. Once the two end uprights are in place attach the center upright. Finally, add the other four uprights.

5 Trim the uprights to a pleasant curve, as shown in figure 2. Use the narrower willow saplings to add a loose and varied band of

Figure 2

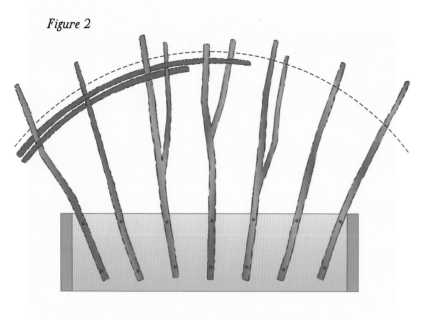

Adding Twig Work and Finishing

6 Begin adding the twig work to the box at the corners, holding two twigs together at each corner and nailing them in place. To avoid splitting the twigs, don't nail too close to their ends. Then add the top and bottom framing twigs, twigs to hide the joints in the bark, and twigs to frame the diamonds. Finally, add decorative designs in the center section and on the box ends.

7 Finish the box by applying exterior polyurethane. Use a clear finish, not one that's amber, to retain the color of the white birch bark.

weaving to the top of the trellis. Nail the weavers to the uprights where necessary to secure them, and trim any excess willow.

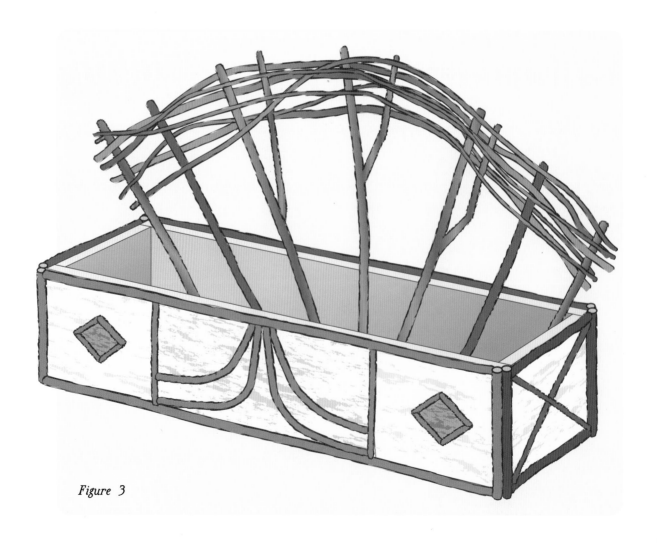

Figure 3

BARK! *By Daniel Mack*

FOUND BARK

If the look you want is gnarly, rough, and uneven, then found bark from fallen trees might be right. This bark has probably dried in the curved shape of the tree and has a certain "memory" of that shape, which will keep it from lying very flat. It will also have discoloration, speckling, and tears. It may have wood decaying on its underside. Bark like this is easiest to locate and has a strong woodland charm. It is difficult to glue down and responds best to mechanical pressure: staples and branches or flattened twigs holding it tight against the structure beneath it.

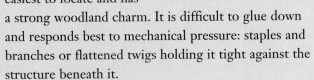

Learning just the basics of birch (or cherry) bark will help you decide what quality and character bark to acquire and how to handle it.

FRESH HARVESTED

This bark is carefully peeled from a living tree by scoring the tree with a sharp knife just down to the inner bark but not to the sapwood. You then remove the bark slowly in long, wide sheets and immediately flatten it and allow it to dry. One method of drying is to staple the very outer edges of the bark to a piece of plywood. Stack such pieces on each other with clean cardboard in between to absorb the moisture. Restack every few weeks to help circulate air and prevent mold from growing. The bark is dry when it has shrunk so much that it has pulled away from the staples.

Even this fresh, flat bark has varying characteristics: bark from the lowest part of the tree or from large-diameter trees can be very thick and leathery and dark in color. Such bark requires both adhesives and mechanical fastening and still retains an earthy feel even in the most careful of applications.

Bark from the middle and upper parts of the tree is thinner, more flexible, and usually whiter. This bark behaves more like veneer.

WHITE BIRCH BARK THAT DELAMINATES

Birch bark grows in layers, like an onion, and sometimes, for various reasons, delaminates into many tissue-thin layers after it is dry. Only the very outside layer retains the original white or silvery quality. The many inner layers are chalky tones of white, cream, pink, sometimes purple, and beige-brown. Some users look for this kind of bark, appreciate the subtle tones, and work with them the way a painter would use different tones of paint. The advantage of delaminated bark is its thinness, which responds very well to tight surface application. But for other users and applications, delaminated bark—or bark that delaminates after application—represents tragedy. Examine your bark for evidence of delamination before you use it.

ADHESIVES

On wavy, leathery bark, I have used heavy, gooey construction adhesives in conjunction with staples and split branches to hold it in place. I expect to get only about 60 to 70 percent of the surfaces glued to each other.

On medium density bark, I have successfully used a water-based contact cement, but this is very sensitive to temperature and proper clamping, much like veneering.

On delaminated bark, I have used a wood glue or spray adhesive. With all adhesives, be alert to bleed-through onto the surface, and use as little as possible.

TOOLS

A paper cutter, T-square, matte knife, sheetrock knife, scissors, tin snips, mat cutter, and a brayer (to roll and pressure the glued bark onto the substrate) can all be helpful tools when working with bark.

Experiment, Experiment, Experiment!

POLE AND PAPER LAMP

Designed by Jim Cunningham

*H*ere's a rustic paper-shaded lamp that will cast a subdued light on your porch or covered patio. It takes a little time to put together, but the results are so stunning, you'll want to let it glow in your den all winter.

MATERIALS

Corner posts: 4 peeled limbs,
1" diameter x 14"

Crosspieces: 8 peeled sticks,
⅝" diameter x 7"

Panel sticks: 12 peeled sticks,
⅜" diameter x 12"

Lid crosspieces: 2 peeled sticks,
⅝" diameter x 7"

Lid panel sticks: 3 peeled sticks,
⅜" diameter x 4½"

Lamp platform: 1½" pine or
hardwood square, 5" x 5"

4 pieces papyrus paper or heavy rice paper,
about 6" x 12"

1 piece papyrus paper or heavy rice paper,
about 6" x 6"

4 brass braising rods, ⅛" diameter x 2"

Candelabra lamp socket fixture, cord, inline
switch, and plug

40- to 60-watt candelabra-size bulb

SUPPLIES & TOOLS

⅜" dowel (optional)

Masking tape

0000 steel wool

Handsaw

Utility knife with new blades

Polymerized tung oil finish

Wipe-on polyurethane finish

Drill with ⅛", ¼", ⅜", and ½" brad point bits

Woodworker's glue or slow-setting epoxy

Large rubber band or web clamp or string

White craft glue

Rasp or rough file

Sharp knife

Belt sander (optional)

Vise or Bar clamp

Drill press (optional)

Tenon cutter (optional)

Spray bottle

Ruler

Hacksaw

Drill press (optional)

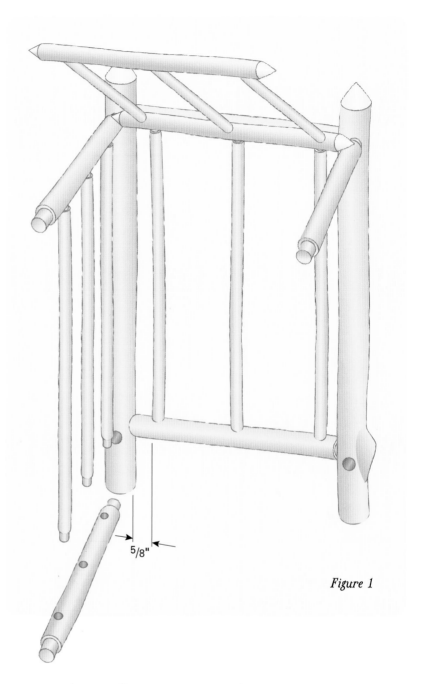

Figure 1

Making the Framework

1 Use a handsaw to cut four 1"-diameter
limbs 14" long. These will be the corner
posts, so try to saw their bottom ends straight
across so the posts will stand level. Shape the
top end of each post into a shallow point by
using a sharp knife, or a rasp and a knife, or by
belt sanding (as Jim Cunningham did) and then
whittling off the sanding marks. Mark the position of each post on its bottom end (FL = front
left, for instance), and draw arrows indicating
the two sides where the mortises will be drilled.

These arrows will be at right angles to one another.

2 Measure up from the bottom on those two sides and mark at 2" and 12" (see figure 1 on page 45). At those marks, drill ⅜"-diameter holes ½" deep. To make sure that your holes will line up, use a vise or clamp to hold the limb so one pair of the marks is right on top. Then drill straight down, using a power drill or drill press. To make sure that the second pair of holes will be at right angles to the first pair, push a ⅜" dowel into one of the first holes, and prop its end so that the dowel is level. Then drill straight down at each mark. If you don't have a dowel lying around, cut one of the ⅜" tenons in the next step, and use that stick as your guide.

3 Cut eight ⅝"-diameter sticks 7" long for crosspieces. Make ⅜"-diameter tenons, ½" long, on each end of the crosspieces. The hardwood tenon sizer described on page 20 works perfectly for these small tenons. Temporarily assemble the lamp framework, arranging the crosspieces for the most pleasing effect.

Adding the Panel Sticks

4 On each crosspiece, mark the centers of the three mortises for the panel sticks. One mortise goes in the middle of each crosspiece, and the other two are ⅜" from the posts (see figure 1).

5 Cut twelve ⅜"-diameter sticks for panel sticks, 11" or 12" long. Whittle a ¼"-diameter x ⅜" long tenon on one end of each panel stick.

6 Take your framework apart, marking each joint as you go so that you can reassemble it the same way. Drill ¼" mortises in the crosspieces at all of your marks, making sure the mortises line up.

7 Reassemble one side of the framework, two posts and two crosspieces. Decide which three panel sticks will go on that side, arrange them, and push their tenon ends into the proper mortises, so that the other ends lay against the other crosspiece. Mark the panel sticks for length, halfway through the crosspiece. Then trim the panels sticks to length, and whittle the tenons. Disassemble the side enough to put the panel sticks in place, making sure that everything fits.

8 Mark the panel sticks as you take the side apart. Then use a rasp or a belt sander to make a narrow flat area along the back of each panel stick to provide a place to glue the paper.

9 Repeat steps 7 and 8 to fit the panel sticks on each of the remaining three sides.

Making the Lid

10 When you're done, reassemble the framework to measure for the lid pieces. You don't have to make a lid, but it does finish the lamp nicely. Lay two ⅝"-diameter sticks

across the top of the framework, leaving a ½" space between them and the posts. Mark them at the centerlines of the crosspieces or a little longer, and cut them to length. Point both ends of these lid crosspieces as you did the top ends of the posts (see figure 1 on page 45).

11 Return the lid crosspieces to the top of the lamp, making sure they lie evenly, cradled by the upper crosspieces. Lay three ⅜" sticks across the lid crosspieces so that two are just inside the pointed sections and one is in the middle. Mark them for length, halfway through the crosspieces. As you remove the lid panel sticks, mark positions for their mortises on the lid crosspieces. Cut the lid panel sticks to length, and whittle their tenons. Bore the mortises in the crosspieces, make sure everything fits, and flatten the backs of the panel sticks, as you did before.

Applying the Finish

12 This is the best time to finish all the pieces of the lamp, because you can work on them easily, without getting finish where it shouldn't go. Use masking tape to protect the tenons where they'll go into the mortises. Rub the sticks with 0000 steel wool to burnish and clean them. Apply one coat of polymerized tung oil finish and three coats of wipe-on polyurethane, following the manufacturers' directions. It's hard to delay the final assembly, but take your time, let each coat dry, and remember that the rest will go much easier.

Assembling the Lamp

13 Now you can start gluing things together, beginning with the panels and the lid. Don't glue anything to the corner posts yet. Lay out all your pieces in assembly order. You can use woodworker's glue if your joints are tight, but epoxy provides a stronger bond. Mix a small amount of epoxy on a plastic lid, and spread it in the mortises of the crosspieces and

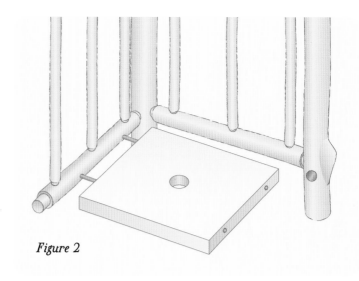

Figure 2

the lid crosspieces. Assemble all the parts, making sure that the flat sides of the panel sticks line up on the inside of the lamp. (Remember: leave the corner posts unglued at this point.) Use a large rubber band or a web clamp or a string tourniquet to hold the framework together. Put the lid on top, clamping it together if necessary. Then weight the whole structure with bricks or books to hold it flat on the table. Let the woodworker's glue or epoxy cure overnight.

14 Remove the panels from the posts, and lay them and the lid on the table, flat sides up. Find that papyrus or rice paper you squirreled away. Frank Cunningham likes the papyrus paper for its strength and texture. Cut the paper a little oversize, past the outer panel pieces and to the centers of the crosspieces. Find the good side of the paper, which will go against the sticks. Mist the back side of the paper with water in the spray bottle, blotting up any excess. This softens the paper and allows it to shrink tight as it dries. Spread a small amount of white craft glue on the flats of the panel sticks and where the paper will roll up onto the crosspieces. Lay the paper in place, and rub it down lightly, moving out from the center. Keep rubbing until the glue begins to hold, usually a few minutes. Before the glue

dries completely, use a utility knife with a new blade to trim the edges.

15 One more bit of building remains: the platform for the light fixture. Drill a ⅜" hole through the center of the wooden square. Switch to a ⅛" bit, hold the square in a vise and drill the holes for the brass rods in opposite edges of the platform piece (see figure 2). These holes are 1" deep, centered thicknesswise on the edge and 1" from the corners. Use a hacksaw to cut four 2" pieces of ⅛" brass rod, and press them into the holes.

16 Now you must dry-assemble the lamp one last time. With the lamp upside down, lay the rod ends on the lower crosspieces, centering the platform in the frame, and mark the positions of the pins on the two crosspieces. Turn the lamp over, and use the ruler to mark the centers of the rod holes, all at the same height from the table. Take the lamp apart enough to drill the holes to accommodate the pins. Make sure that the pins in the platform fit the holes in the crosspieces, and widen the holes or bend the pins if necessary. Mark the pieces so that you can put them back together the same way. Wire and install the lamp socket, remembering to thread the cord through the hole first. Use an inline switch.

17 Final assembly time, at last! Lay out the posts and the panels in order, mix up your epoxy, spread it in the post mortises, and reassemble the lamp, putting the platform in place as you do. Pull the pieces together as before, weighting the top, and waiting a few hours, at least, before imparting a soft glow to your patio.

Figure 3

MOSAIC TWIG TABLE

Designed by Tor Faegre

*V*isually complicated but easy to make, this table exemplifies the rustic ethos. Find the right materials *and invent your own pattern for the top.*

MATERIALS

Tabletop: 1¼" exterior plywood oval,
18" x 28"

Table edge trim: 3 willow branches,
⅜" to ½" diameter x 7' (or 6 shorter pieces)

Legs: 4 curved limbs with branches, 2½" x 24"

Twig work: willow (or other) twigs,
⅜" to ½" diameter

SUPPLIES & TOOLS

1" to 1¼" brown paneling nails

2½" and 1⅝" decking or drywall screws

Band saw or saber saw

Hammer

Pruning shears

Drill with #2 Philips driver

Level

Small saw

Assembling the Top and Legs

1 Lay out and cut an 18" x 28" oval from ¾" exterior plywood, or have it cut for you.

2 Trim the edge of the plywood by nailing three bands of ⅜"- to ½"-diameter willow branches in the following order: First, a bottom band flush with the bottom of the plywood.

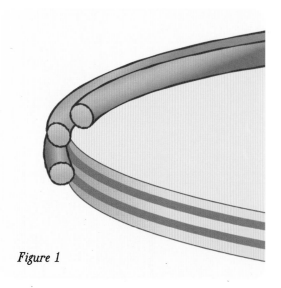

Figure 1

Next, a band directly above the first. Finally, another branch nailed to the top surface tight against the second band (see figure 1). Start your bands at different places around the edge so the joints don't coincide. If your willow is too short, cut its end at a long angle, and cut the next piece to match. Nail twice through the joint where the ends overlap. If you want to get fancy, cut a similar joint where the far end meets the beginning end.

3 If you can find some curved limbs with smaller branches growing from them, you're in great shape, because you can use the branches as built-in supports for the legs. If you have only nicely curved limbs for legs, you can screw branches to them to serve as stretchers, as Tor Faegre did in the table pictured. Decide how tall your table will be, and allow some extra length on the legs. Cut the top of your legs so that they fit flat against the bottom of the plywood. Arrange them so they look good and so that any branches contact other legs or the plywood. Then shoot two or three 2½" screws through the top of the plywood into the top of each leg.

4 Use shorter screws to attach the branches so that they brace the legs.

5 Find a level surface and put the table on it; then put a spirit level on top of the table. Use shims under the legs to level the plywood. Decide exactly how tall the table will be, and find a block of wood for a guide to mark the bottoms of the legs. Lay a pencil on the block, and move both on the level surface to draw a line around each leg. Use a small saw to cut to the lines.

Decorating the Top

6 Sketch a pattern for the top. You might begin with sticks following the curve of the edge and add pieces aligned with the long and

short axes of the oval, as the designer did. He then bent several twigs to the outside curve of each quadrant and filled the rest of the space from the inside with straight pieces. Use pruning shears to cut the twig ends at an angle, so that they fit nicely against the twigs they bump into (see figure 2). Nail each twig as you go to get a tight fit between twigs.

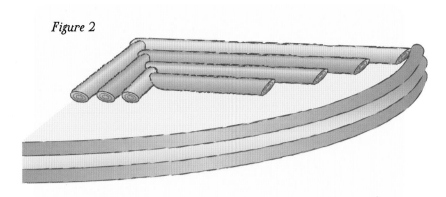

Figure 2

7 Here are some more design options for the top: Use different colors or different species to build additional patterns of texture. You could fill the entire oval with swirling or wavy lines. Start with one bent twig and add more on either side of it until the surface is full. You might even group the thicker ends of twigs to emphasize the curves. While a flat surface might seem most appropriate for a tabletop, consider using a gradation of twig sizes to produce intentional "troughs" or "hollows." Let your imagination run wild.

Figure 3

Designed by Andy Rae

SLAB DESK

*ow inspiring would it be to write your novel—or
your shopping list—on the patio? This desk, combining two very different but complementary woods, provides a
perfect platform for thinking outside the box.*

MATERIALS

Top: 1 bark-edged plank, at least 15" wide x at least 40"

Legs: 4 small peeled limbs, 1¼" to 2" diameter x 30"

Stretchers: 2 or 3 peeled sticks, ⅝" to ¾" diameter

Hardwood for wedges

*Note: Check local sawmills for wild grain patterns in the
plank for the top of this desk. But keep in mind that the wood
must be well dried before you have it planed. Wild grain
often translates as wacky warpage in the drying process.
Better to deal with that before you start adding legs! The legs
and stretchers should be dry, too.*

SUPPLIES & TOOLS

Oil finish

Trimming saw

Drill with a variety of bits

Tenon cutter

Knife and/or chisel

Round file or suitable gouge

Backsaw or dozuki saw

Level

Cutting the Desk Mortises

1 Begin by propping the top plank a foot or so higher
than the finished height of the desk. Choose your legs
by leaning likely candidates against the top or by wedging
them in place under the plank. Andy used a long, thin
branch from one leg as a stretcher to the other back leg.
You can add a stretcher stick in its place if your limbs
don't have branches. Mark the legs and their positions so
you'll remember where they go.

2 Once you've chosen your leg pieces, cut them 3" or 4" longer than the table height (29" to 30" for a writing table). The tops of the legs go through the tabletop and are wedged in place. Determine the tenon diameter for the legs. This will be somewhat smaller than the thinnest leg. Since the wedges are intended to draw the tenons through the mortises, you'll need a small shoulder around each tenon.

3 Mark the centers of the four legs on the bottom of the top plank. An old-fashioned brace and bit works well for boring these holes, because the screw center breaks the top surface well ahead of the cutting spurs, allowing you to finish the hole from the top side of the plank. That prevents the wood around the hole from tearing away. Use the leg, held upside down near the mark, to indicate the proper angle for the hole. Bore partway through the plank and then finish the hole from the plank's top surface.

Cutting the Leg Tenons

4 Use a tenon cutter or a knife to cut the tenons on the tops of the legs. The tenons should be a little longer than the thickness of the top plank. Push a tenon into its mortise, hold it at the intended angle, and mark a shoulder with a sharp pencil held flat against the underside of the top. Mark all the way around the leg. Extend the tenon to the shoulder depth with a knife or a chisel, keeping the shoulder perpendicular to the tenon. Repeat for the other legs.

Adding the Stretchers

5 Put the legs in place and stand the table upright. You may need to put spacers under some legs to maintain their positions. Choose and arrange stretchers for each end and the back of the table. Use spring clamps, string, rubber bands, or tape to hold them against the

legs until the arrangement pleases you. Then mark their lengths and their positions on the legs. Make an "X" where each mortise will be bored. Allow enough length on the stretchers for their tenons to penetrate at least halfway through the legs.

6 Drill mortise holes with the legs still in position, if you can. Otherwise, rotate the legs only enough to get the correct angle. Use the stretcher sticks to help gauge the angles.

7 Trim the stretchers to length, and cut or whittle the tenons. Assemble the legs and stretchers, and replace the top onto the leg tenons.

Preparing the Wedged Tenons

8 Once everything fits, mark for saw kerfs on the ends of the leg tenons. These lines should run perpendicular to the grain of the top and be centered on each tenon. Extend the lines onto the top plank to indicate how to widen the tops of the mortises. (See page 21 for more information and photos of wedged tenons.)

9 Remove the top, and saw down to $\frac{1}{8}$" above the shoulder on each tenon. Use a round file to widen the tops of the mortises in the top plank. Avoid rounding the sides of the holes—if you do, the wedges won't fill the gaps. Don't touch the areas around your marks from the previous step. Remove at most $\frac{1}{16}$" from two opposite sides of each hole.

10 Figure out how fat your wedges should be. They have to fill the kerf and the spaces you just made without bottoming out in the kerf. Make at least four wedges the width of the tenons. Resist the temptation to try the fit of the wedges. All you can possibly discover is that they fit so well you can't get them out.

Gluing and Assembling the Desk

11 Take everything apart, think pure thoughts, and start gluing and assembling. Start with the stretchers, one joint at a time, until the top can go on. Put the top on the tenons without glue until you secure the glued joints with clamps or twine or arm power. Remove the top, glue its joints, and replace it. Squeeze some glue into a tenon kerf, and start its wedge. Grab the leg, lift it a little, and hammer the wedge home, watching to see that the top seats against the shoulder around the tenon. Do the same with the other three wedges.

12 When the glue has cured, trim the ends of the tenons flush with the tabletop, using a backsaw or dozuki saw. Sand those areas (and the whole top if you haven't done so already). You can apply the first coat of finish to the top now.

13 Working on a flat surface, put spacers under the legs until the top is parallel with the working surface. Use a level for this only if your working surface is also level! Measure the height of the table propped up, and subtract the intended height of the table—that's the height of the spacer block you'll need to trim the bottoms of the legs. Find or make a suitable spacer, lay a pencil flat on top of it, and draw trimming lines all around each leg. Saw to the lines. You may still have a little judicious trimming to do as the legs settle into place, but go ahead with your finishing so you can start writing that rustic novel!

Figure 1

55

FOLDING SCREEN

Designed by Kevin Barnes

*T*he zigzag design of this rustic screen allows it to stand in any spot where you want to add visual interest. Go as crazy as you dare with the panel saplings. This is frame and panel construction at its quick-
est, so take time to gather inspiring material.

MATERIALS

Posts: 6 straight hardwood saplings, 2" diameter x 6½'

Crosspieces: 12 hardwood sticks, 1" diameter x 18"

Panel pieces: 12 hardwood saplings (with branches) at least 6½' long

4 leather strips, 2" x 12"

SUPPLIES & TOOLS

Headed nails

Saw

Lopper

Hammer

Building the Screen

1 Cut the posts and crosspieces to length. While the height of the posts can vary, the crosspieces should all be the same length.

2 For each section of the screen, lay two posts on your work surface so that they're parallel, 15" apart on center, with their bottom ends even. Lay two crosspieces on the posts, one 6" up from the bottoms and the other 5½' above the first. Nail the crosspieces to the posts.

3 Turn the frame over, and lay in four panel saplings with their bottom ends extending 1" or so beyond the bottom crosspiece. You should arrange the panel pieces for the other two panels now, so that the overall effect will be balanced. When you're pleased with your arrangement, nail the panel saplings to the crosspieces.

4 Lay a crosspiece directly above each of the installed crosspieces, and nail the new ones to the posts.

5 When you've assembled the three sections, choose the center one, and nail one end of each of the leather strips to its posts. These hinges go 6" below the upper crosspieces and an equal distance above the lower ones. Use

headed nails such as copper tacks for fastening the leather. Loop the strips around the post of the next panel and back around the first post to overlap the nails. Make sure that the sections can fold nearly flat, and nail the leather strips in place. Attach the hinges for the third section in the same way.

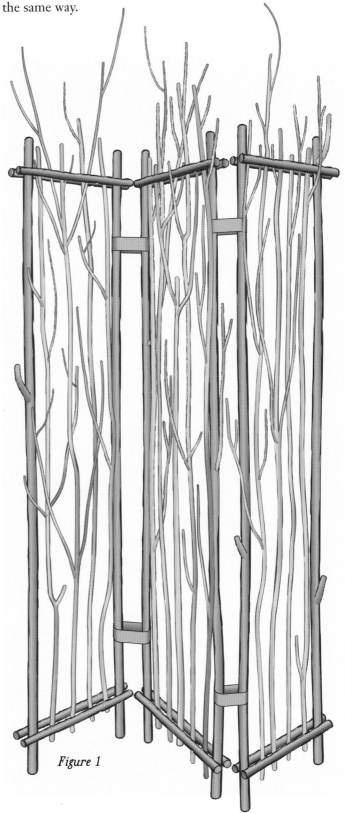

Figure 1

LARGE LUMINARY

Designed by Cheryl Evans

Here's a soft light to welcome guests to your garden. It goes together so quickly that you'll want to make more than one. Find a good supply of alder or willow saplings, and go to town.

MATERIALS

Saplings: 45 to 55 alder saplings
½" to ¾" diameter x 72" to 78"

Sticks: 30 to 40 alder sticks
½" to ¾" diameter x 8"

Bases: 2 squares of ¼" exterior plywood,
12" x 12"

Tomato cage with 12" bottom ring

Rope lights, 6' of clear lights, end cap, mounting clips, and power cord (also available as a complete kit 24' long that can be cut to length)

Strong waxed cord

Sea grass or similar twine

SUPPLIES & TOOLS

1⅝" brown or black paneling nails

1¼" and 2" drywall screws

Black or brown exterior spray paint

Compass

Drill with ⅜" drill bit

Jigsaw

Loppers

Garden pruners

Hammer

Wire cutters

Assembling the Base

1   Cut a 7" diameter hole in the center of each plywood square, as follows: Draw diagonals between opposite corners, and use a compass set to 3½" to draw a circle from the center. Drill a ⅜" hole through the plywood anywhere on the line. Use a jigsaw to cut along the line.

2   Cut along the diagonals of one of the discs removed from the plywood squares to produce four quadrants. Align the edges of the quadrants with the corners of one of the plywood squares, and fasten them with two 1¼" drywall screws each.

3   Paint all the surfaces of both squares with brown or black spray paint. When they're

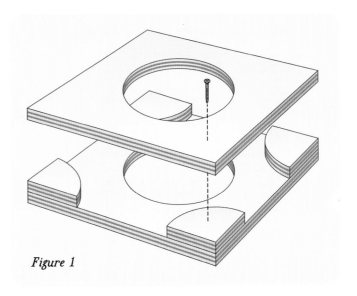

Figure 1

dry, stack the second square on the first, sandwiching the quadrants between them. Align the corners, and fasten the base together with a 2" drywall screw through each quadrant (see figure 1).

4   Now add the lights. Follow the manufacturer's instructions for assembling the rope lights. Start fastening the rope to the base at a corner using the plastic mounting clips and screws. Wind the rope around the square, keeping it about ¼" from the outside edge, and securing it as necessary. When you get back to the first side, continue winding about ¼" inside the first circuit. When you've secured the lights, let the cord dangle through the hole.

Building the Luminary

5   As you add the alder saplings to the base, remember to cut their fat ends square before you nail them in place. Choose a long sapling, and align its edge with a corner of the base so that 5" of its fat end extends beyond the bottom of the base for a leg. Use two paneling nails to secure it, one in each layer of the base. Add a sapling to the other side at the same corner, and do the same at the other three corners (see figure 2 on page 60).

pieces until you reach the middle of a side (see figure 3).

10 When you finish nailing sticks and saplings to a side, tie the saplings to the wire square. Then go on to the next side.

11 Add a decorative touch by weaving sea grass or similar heavy twine in and out of the saplings just above the sticks until you have a 1"-wide band. You can weave above the wire square, too, or decide that the cord ties offer enough visual interest.

12 Use waxed cord to gather the saplings into a tight circle about 42" from the bottom of the luminary. Straighten them as you tighten the cord. You may find that they want to twist as a group, but make sure they don't distort the structure. Wrap the cord around the saplings several times, and tie it securely. You can wrap over the cords with sea grass if you wish.

13 You can leave your luminary outdoors if you've used rope lights intended for exterior use, but it will last longer if you store it under cover on a dry floor.

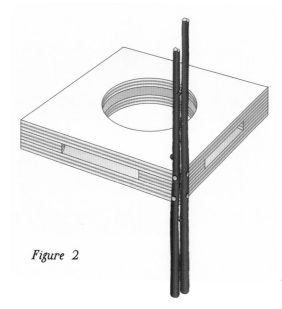

Figure 2

6 Add another long sapling next to each of the eight corner saplings, aligning their bottom ends. Stand the luminary on a table and trim the legs if it doesn't stand straight.

7 Remove the bottom ring from a tomato cage using wire cutters. Mark a point anywhere on the ring, and measure around the ring 9". Mark that spot and continue around the ring until you have four marks equally spaced. You may have to adjust your marks a bit, but don't get too fussy. Using those marks as the corners, straighten the wire between them until you have a square.

8 Measure 26" up from the bottom of the saplings and mark them. Hold the wire square inside the saplings at your marks, and tie the saplings to the wire with waxed cord. Wrap the cord to make an "X" on the outside of each sapling, and tie the ends tightly. Start at one corner, tying the two adjacent saplings, then do the same at the opposite corner. You'll be pulling the saplings inward as you go.

9 The rest of the sticks and saplings begin ¼" above the bottoms of the legs. Add an 8" stick and a sapling to those already in place at each corner of the base, alternating the

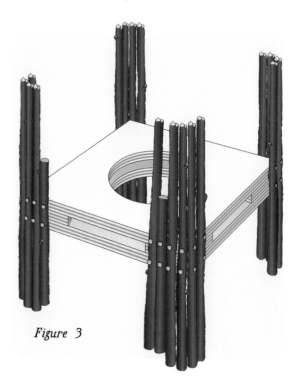

Figure 3

This chair mimics the form of a classic Adirondack chair, but its joinery is more sophisticated. This project shows how rustic materials lend themselves to more individual and expressive statements than most furniture made from flat planks. Consider letting some branch stubs protrude from the posts and stretchers.

ADIRONDACK CHAIR

Designed by Brian Creelman

MATERIALS

Front posts: 2 peeled white cedar limbs, 2¾" diameter x 21¼"

Side seat rails: 2 peeled white cedar limbs, 2½" diameter x 37"

Back posts: 2 peeled white cedar limbs, 2½" diameter x 26"

Arms: 2 peeled white cedar slabs, 2" x 7" to 8" x 27¾"

Front seat stretcher: 1 peeled white cedar limb, 2¼" diameter x 24"

Lower front stretcher: 1 peeled white cedar limb, 1½" diameter x 24"

Rear seat stretcher: 1 peeled white cedar limb, 2½" diameter x 24"

Bottom back stretcher: 1 peeled white cedar limb, 2½" diameter x 24"

Crest rail: 1 peeled white cedar limb, 2¾" diameter x 26"

Seat slats: 5 boards or flitches, 1" x 3¾" x 20"

Back slats: 5 boards or flitches, 1" x 3¾" x 36"

Note: Brian Creelman makes this chair from spring-peeled, seasoned Eastern white cedar saplings harvested from a dense stand of young cedar trees. The arms come from slab offcuts obtained at a local sawmill. Rough lumber could be substituted. "Flitches" are bark-to-bark planks sawn from small cedar trees to produce an irregular profile.

SUPPLIES & TOOLS

Epoxy

Microfibers

2" to 2½" copper or silicon bronze ring nails

Oil finish

Saw

Hammer

Adjustable bevel

1" and 1½" tenon cutters

Drill with 1" and 1½" drill bits

Block plane or bench plane

Pipe clamps or long bar clamps

Drawknife

Assembling the Side Panels

Note: All tenons in the side panel assembly are 1½" diameter x 1¾" long, measured to the extent of the cove shoulder. While you can cut the pieces for both sides at the same time, remember that the two sides mirror each other. These instructions describe the assembly of one side.

It will be helpful to make a full-size drawing of the side view, as shown in figure 1. Then you can lay your pieces on the drawing to make sure of mortise positions and angles. Don't worry if your stock is a little bigger or smaller than the drawing—this is rustic work, after all—just align the centerlines of the pieces.

1 Cut the front post to length, and cut a tenon on its top end.

2 Attach 4" x 4" plywood end blocks, as described in End Blocks for Accurate Joinery (page 18). Mark and drill the front post's mortise for the side seat rail 12" from the bottom of the post. Lift the angle from the drawing.

3 Cut the side seat rail to length, and shape a tenon on its front end. Attach an end block to the back end. Don't cut the "foot" portion yet. Push the tenon into its mortise, and lay the assembly on your drawing to lift off the mortise location for the back post and its angle. Then cut the mortise.

4 Cut the back post to length, and cut a tenon on each end. Assemble the three side pieces so that you can find the mortise location and angle for the arm, and drill the hole.

5 Now find slab pieces for the arms. They should be approximately equal to each other in thickness, and their thicker ends should be in front. It's nice if the back ends of the arms are just over 1½" thick to fill the mortise with-

Figure 1

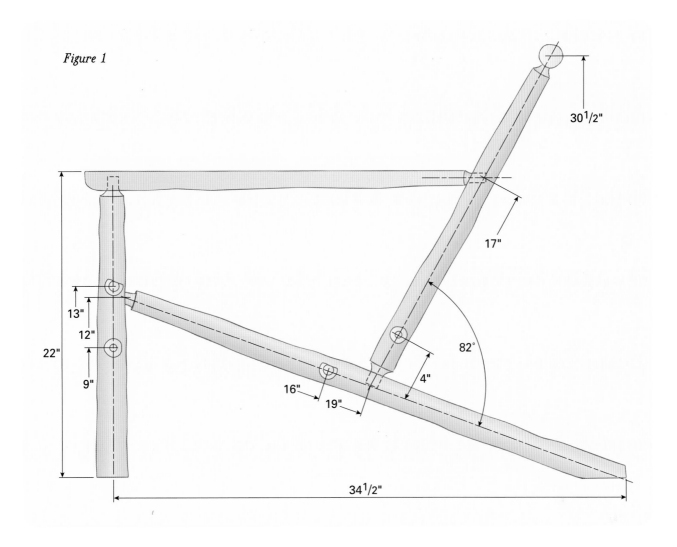

out producing an overly dramatic shoulder. Plane off any sharp corners on the inside edge to establish a reference face and to make the arm more comfortable in use. Draw a centerline on the face of the arm, and square from that line to draw the ends of the arm. Cut the arm to length. To establish the position of the tenon, draw a line parallel with the centerline and 2" from the inside edge. That will be the center-line of the tenon. Whittle the back end of the arm enough to allow your tenon cutter to shape a tenon, and cut the tenon.

6 The line you drew to locate the tenon also marks the center of the mortise for the front post, so square the line down the front end of the arm, and connect it on the bottom surface to the tenon's center. There's probably enough play in the joints to allow marking the

mortise directly. Twist the arm tenon into its mortise in the back post, make sure that the posts and rail match the drawing, and mark the position of the front post tenon, about 2" from the front of the arm. Bore the mortise where the two lines cross.

7 Shape the edges of the arm as shown in figure 2 on page 64, and remember to trace the first arm on the second arm with their faces together to produce a right and a left side.

8 Glue the first side together using epoxy thickened to syrup consistency with microfibers. Then go ahead and make the second side, comparing it to the first to avoid racking in the final chair assembly.

2"

Figure 2

Connecting the Side Panels with Stretchers.

9 Transfer the stretcher mortise positions from the drawing onto the inside of the side panels. Note that the mortises for the front seat stretcher are 1" diameter, while the others measure 1½". This prevents that stretcher mortise from unduly weakening the side seat rail tenon where the joints overlap. Drill the mortises in the side panels.

10 Now you must measure for each stretcher individually, because the side panel pieces are irregular. If you make all the stretchers the same size, invariably one or two will keep the others from seating properly, and that produces a cockeyed chair. So stand the two side panels on your worktable, plumb and 22" from centerline to centerline. You might want to clamp or screw the front post end blocks to the table, measuring between the centers of the blocks. Then adjust the back ends, and make sure the side panels stand perpendicular to the table. Lay a piece of plywood against the fronts of the back posts above the arms, and clamp it to keep the sides steady. Recheck your measurements between the centers of the blocks and between the centers of the back post tenons. Measure the distance between the sides at each stretcher location, add 3½", and mark your stretcher stock, both for length and to identify each piece. Notice that the lower front stretcher is only 1½" in diameter.

11 Cut the stretchers to length, and cut the crest rail while you're at it. Cut 1½"

tenons on both ends of the stretchers except for the lower front, which gets 1" tenons.

12 The lower front stretcher is ready to use, but the other stretchers and the crest rail must be shaped. Plane the seat stretchers flat on one side to the level of the tenons. Use a drawknife to make a concave surface on the front sides of the bottom back stretcher and the crest rail. The concave surface will be about 19" long and have a radius of 40" or so. That means that its center will be recessed about 1¼". Try for a fair curve without any flat areas. You might want to make a pattern to help visualize where to remove the wood.

13 When the stretchers have been shaped, assemble the chair to check for fit. This is a good time to mark and bore the crest rail mortises. Use a long straight edge to align the concave surfaces of the bottom back stretcher and the crest rail. Then take it all apart, apply thickened epoxy inside the mortises, reassemble the chair, and clamp across the side panels. Remember to align the seat stretcher flats.

14 As soon as you have the sides clamped to the stretchers, and you've made sure that the sides are perpendicular to the table again, glue the crest rail in place. Align those concave surfaces again!

15 Instead of just sitting there watching the glue cure, prop the front posts on 1" spacers, and use another 1"-thick piece of wood with a pencil held flat on top to mark the angled cut on the bottom of the side seat rails. Cut to the lines when you can lay the chair on its side.

Adding the Seat and Back Slats

16 If you're using planks for your slats, cut them to length, and taper them from

3¾" at one end (tops of the back slats and fronts of the seat slats) to 3" at the other end. If you're using flitches, select them for a strong taper approximating those dimensions.

17 Lay the chair on its back so that the crest rail is close to the edge of the worktable. Center one back slat on the back stretcher and crest rail, and use a straightedge to align its bottom end with the seat stretchers. Nail the center slat in place temporarily. Arrange the other slats to form a nice, subtle fan shape, keeping their bottom ends just below the level of the seat stretchers. Nail them temporarily, as well.

18 Draw a straight line across the bottoms of the slats at the level of the seat stretchers. Use your concave surface pattern to draw a 40" radius arc across the tops of the slats. You didn't make that pattern? Then use a spline (a thin piece of wood or a flexible ruler) to draw an arc. In either case, make sure that the ends of the line land at equal heights and that the top of the curve is at the centerline of the middle slat.

19 Follow a similar procedure to fit the seat slats. There's one extra step here: when you arrange each of the four side slats, mark and cut its back end parallel with the back slat it butts against. Then nail it in place and go on to the next slat. The fronts of the seat slats can be cut in a straight line across the chair, or you can draw a shallow convex curve, and cut to that.

20 Remove the slats, and cut their ends. Sand them if you wish, but be sure to round all the edges a little bit. If you plan to finish your chair, do so now, before you assemble it into a mess of skinny spaces and tight crevasses.

21 Nail the slats in place with 2" to 2½" copper or silicon bronze ring nails. Boat builders use these nails to attach bottom planking, so you know they hold tightly for a long time. One nail at each stretcher, driven through the same holes as before, will do the trick. If you had cut off the bottom corners of the side seat rails before, you'd be done now. To protect the legs from moisture, coat the bottoms of the front posts and the side seat rails with a heavy dose of epoxy. And don't put the chair on the porch until that epoxy has cured, okay? Nice going! Now you're done.

Figure 3

LIVING LOVESEAT

Designed by Kim Vergil

*B*uild (and plant) this loveseat in spring or late fall. You'll soon have a leafy arbor to enjoy with a friend. Consider planting colorful climbers like morning glories, red runner beans, or honeysuckle around the chair to add color to the canopy.

MATERIALS

Back rods: 20 willow branches, ¾" to 1" diameter x 10' to 12'

Front rods: 11 willow branches, ¾" to 1" diameter x 30"

Weavers: approximately 250 willow branches, ½" to ¾" x 5'

Cedar chips

Flat stones or wood slabs for seat

SUPPLIES & TOOLS

2 pieces of ½" plywood or MDF, 26" x 60"

4 2 x 4s, 10" long

String

2" drywall screws

Drill with 1¼" bit

Loppers

Pruning shears

Building the Weaving Jig

1 The weaving jig holds all the rods to make your weaving easy and regular. Stack the two pieces of plywood on top of each other. Lay out the centers of the 1¼" holes by following the plan in figure 1, where each square equals 1". Drill all the holes through both layers of plywood.

2 Drive screws through the plywood to secure the 2 x 4 spacers at the corners of the jig, as shown in figure 2 on page 68.

3 Place the jig on the floor in a spot where you will be able to leave it until you finish the weaving. Put the front rods in the 11 center front slots. The space under the top of the weaving jig represents the depth the rods will be buried when you plant your loveseat. Put the long back rods in the remaining holes. Trim the tops of the long rods and remove all side

Figure 1

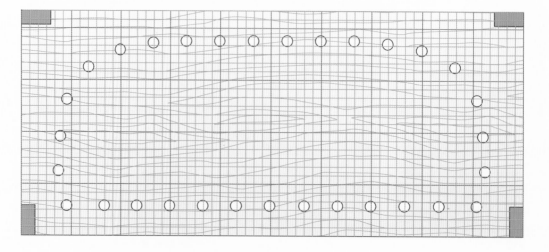

branches to encourage new growth once new roots have been established.

Beginning the Arches

4 Bend the tops of the two corner rods toward each other, and wrap them together so they make an arch about 70" high, measured from the top of the jig. Tie each end to the opposite rod with a short piece of string. Bend the next two back rods, and connect them in the same way to form a slightly shorter arch. Then do the same with the third pair.

5 About halfway up the arches, begin a band of temporary stabilizing weaving. Beginning on one side at the front, leave at least 6" of weaver protruding while you weave in-and-out as far as you can. Start another weaver in the same way but on the other side of the first rod. Weave the protruding ends back in to hold the first rod in place. Insert two more weavers starting from the other side. Maintain the 4" spacing of the rods.

Weaving the Basket Seat

6 Begin at any rod at the top of the jig. Always using two weavers at once, start a twisted-pair weave around the loveseat base. See figure 3, which shows how the weaver that is "behind" always goes over the other weaver, behind the next rod, and out again, leaving the

other weaver behind and ready to follow a similar path. Use the entire length of the weavers, sticking the fine ends into the middle. Always start a new pair at least five rods away from the beginning rod of the previous pair. Because you want the butt ends of the weavers to start on the inside of the structure, in effect, the two weavers begin behind two successive rods. As soon as you hold two weavers up to the rods, you'll see what I mean. It's much easier to do than to describe!

7 Continue the twist weave until your weaving is 5" high. Then switch techniques, weaving in-and-out with two weavers together. This creates bold bands of simple weaving. The same rules as before apply here. Start with butt ends on the inside of a rod and at least five rods from where the previous pair began. When the weavers become too fine, tuck them inside, and begin a new pair.

8 Use the paired plain weave until the woven base is 16" high. Then switch back to twisted-pair weaving, going once around left to right, and once around in the opposite direction. You'll need at least two pairs of weavers for each circuit. This time, secure your ends by tucking them down into the weaving next to a rod. Trim the top ends of the front rods.

Finishing the Back

9 Adjust the arches so that the middle arch is tallest, about 72", and the back one is shorter than the front arch. Then remove the stabilizing weavers, and remove the loveseat from the weaving jig.

10 Beginning with the center pair of back rods, cross them, and weave them diagonally until you get to the front (see figure 4). The next pair crosses above the first pair and weaves on the other side of each rod from the first pair. Continue in this fashion until you've

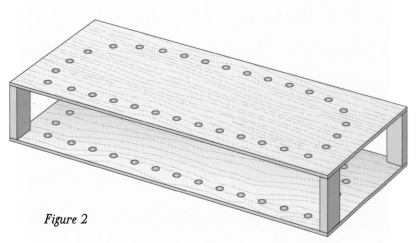

Figure 2

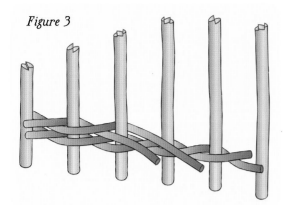

Figure 3

woven all the remaining back rods into a diamond pattern. When you're pleased with the shape of the canopy, wrap and tuck the rod ends into the front arch.

Planting Your Loveseat

11 Try to choose a site with moist soil and good sunlight, but stay away from the foundations of buildings and pools so the roots have plenty of room to grow. Mark a line 6" outside the base of the loveseat, and dig a hole or a trench at least 12" deep.

12 Put the loveseat in the hole, and tilt it backward slightly. Run water into the hole as you begin refilling it with dirt. Fill the hole past its previous level, and tamp it down around the rods.

13 Fill the seat with wood chips, preferably cedar chips, because they resist rotting. Pile the chips nearly to the top of the weaving. Place flat stones or wooden slabs on the chips, and add more chips, stuffing them firmly around the seats. By the way, you can fill the seat with dirt instead of chips if

you want to plant thyme or moss around the stones or slabs.

14 Now, water the loveseat until it has formed roots. Don't let the soil dry out. When I say water, I mean lots of it and often. Curling a soaker hose around the base makes watering more convenient. You can add more wood chips around the base to help retain moisture and discourage weeds. When your chair sends out shoots, you can prune them in the fall, or weave them back in to make the canopy denser.

Figure 4

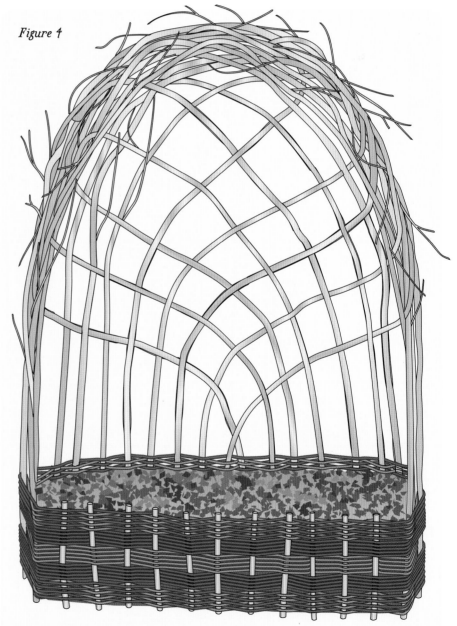

Identifying and Propagating Bush Willows By Kim Vergil

We are all familiar with weeping willow, but we don't weave or build with it because weeping willow has no structural strength in its branches, and it becomes very brittle when it dries. For rustic work, you need to identify any one of the hundred-plus kinds of bush willow or *Salix*.

If you want to make a living structure, you look for willows that flourish in your area. Pussy willow is one kind of bush willow, and it, like other bush willows, grows in wet soil. Look near the banks of rivers and streams, in and around marshes, and by lakes. You can identify willows by their relatively thin leaves that have points at both ends. Often these leaves have silvery, and even velvety, undersides. The leaves turn bright yellow in the fall, and they remain on the stem longer than any other leaves except for oaks. Bush willows can grow to 30' and taller.

Willow branches root very easily because their bark contains high levels of natural rooting hormones. A cut willow branch pushed 8" to 12" into the ground and given lots of sun and water for the first year will root and grow. You can cut several 18" sticks from one willow branch for propagation. Make sure to plant the bottom end of each stick—the bud markings always point upward. The optimum size for propagating sticks is about 1" in diameter. Pound the sticks into the ground if you have to, using a rubber mallet. Trim the top end at an angle to remove any damage and to keep rain from soaking the end. Then water, water, water those plantings.

In the first year the stick will produce one shoot. Allow the shoot to grow for another year to help develop the root system, then cut it back to the ground. The following year you'll see up to 10 new shoots. Early in the next spring, cut most of the shoots back, and leave two to nourish the roots. Soon, the plant will produce 20 to 30 new shoots. Every four to five years, in the early spring before the growth season, you should cut the bush back to its roots. This "coppicing" will keep the bush vigorous and strengthen its root system. If you're serious about growing bush willows, plant them about 1½' apart in rows 3' to 4' apart. This encourages the branches to grow straight and tall to reach the sun.

The best time to plant willow structures or start plantations is right after the frost has left the ground in the spring (if you have ground frost) or during the spring rainy season. You can make a mini-greenhouse by laying a clear or white plastic sheet over the sticks (or over your living structure). Cut several holes for ventilation, and mist inside the plastic to keep it moist but not drenched. Remove the plastic when the leaves appear, but keep watering the plants.

The second best time to plant would be in the late fall, after the leaves have fallen off and the branches have reverted to their dormant state. If you plant in the fall, the sticks can get an early start and take full advantage of the spring rainy season.

STONE TOP BENCH

Designed by Paul Ruhlmann

This impressive bench is actually easy to make. The challenge is to find the stone and drill the four mortise holes in it.

MATERIALS

Top: 1 piece of soft stone (bluestone, limestone), about 2" thick and at least 14" x 32"

Legs: 4 peeled sticks, 1¼" to 1½" diameter and 1" longer than bench height

Long stretchers: 4 peeled sticks, ¾" to 1" diameter and as long as the length of the top

Short stretchers: 4 peeled sticks, ¾" to 1" diameter and as long as the width of the top

⅛" dowel

SUPPLIES & TOOLS

Structural epoxy

Paint (optional)

Small saw

Vise

Drill with ⅛" and ¾" bits and ¾" carbide masonry bit

¾" tenon cutter

Rubber mallet or padded pipe clamps

Web clamp or string tourniquet

Rotary hammer drill (if you can borrow one)

Note: Find the material for your bench top in an odd lot pile at a stone yard. Soft stone such as bluestone or limestone works well, but you can also use wood, cast concrete, or tufa.

Making the Base

1 Decide on a height for your bench. A normal bench will be between 17" and 18" tall. Deduct the thickness of your stone; then add 1" for the top tenons and another 1" for leveling the legs. Cut the four legs to this length.

2 Think of each side of the base as a two-rung ladder. Line up all four legs and mark them for the mortises for the end stretchers. Get the proper splay angle in the legs by mounting each one in a vise, slanted so that the

tenon end is 2" higher than the foot end. All of the tenons in this bench are ¾" diameter and 1" long. Drill straight down at both marks, about 1⅛" deep.

3 The mortises for long rungs and end rungs in the legs should have at least 1" of wood between them, so the centers of mortises on adjacent sides should be 1¾" or more apart. Keeping this spacing in mind, mark the legs for the mortises for the long rungs so that you have two "left" legs and two "right" legs. Bore the mortises for the long stretchers at the same splay angle as before, making sure they are 90 degrees to the end mortises.

4 Lay two legs parallel to each other and nearly as far apart as your stone top is wide. Leaving the foot ends in place, move the tenon ends inwards by 2" each. Lay short stretcher sticks across the legs at the levels of their mortises, and mark them for length, allowing 1" extra on each end for the tenons. Cut the stretchers to length. Hold them level in a vise while you cut a tenon on each end. Repeat this process for all the stretchers.

5 Dry fit the stretchers and the legs, using a rubber mallet or padded pipe clamps to push the parts together. You should be able to twist the structure so that the legs sit evenly on a flat surface. When you are satisfied with the fit, disassemble the base, put glue in the mortises, and put it back together. Use a slow setting structural epoxy, with a suitable thickening material so that the glue stays in place while you add all the stretchers. Use a web clamp or a tourniquet to hold the structure until the glue cures. Reinforce each joint with a ⅛" dowel running through the tenon. (See page 20.)

6 With the base on the floor, cut 1"long tenons on the tops of the legs. Cut them vertically, not in line with the legs.

Cutting the Bench Top Mortises

7 Turn the stone and the base upside down to position the leg tenons. Use a marker to trace the tenons. Use a carbide masonry bit to cut the mortises 1⅛" deep in the stone. Paul Ruhlmann says that a regular drill works fine for this job, but a rotary hammer drill is even better. Apply structural epoxy to the mortises, and push the leg tenons home.

8 When the epoxy has cured, turn the bench right side up on a flat surface, and level the top using shims under the legs, if necessary. Mark the final height of the bench by measur-ing down one leg from the top surface. Find a spacer, such as a piece of scrap wood, that will hold a marker at the level of the mark on the leg. With the marker held on top of the spacer, mark around all the legs, turn the bench over, and cut the legs to length.

9 Paul Ruhlmann likes to paint the bases of his benches. The decorative pattern shown, based on Australian Aboriginal art, consists of meandering rows of paint dots in a contrasting color. See Painting and Finishing Outdoor Furniture on page 121 for more information.

Figure 1

BITTERSWEET CHAIR

Designed by Laura Spector

*F*eeling regal? Know someone who is? Here's the chair for you. Made from Oriental Bittersweet (a plant whose curvy vines will certainly challenge your flexibility), this is a garden seat fit for a queen.

MATERIALS

Legs: 4 straight Oriental Bittersweet vines, 1½" to 2" diameter x 15"

Stretchers: 12 vines, 1¼" to 1¾" diameter x 24"

Seat slats: enough 1"- to 1¼"-diameter vines to cover the seat

Seat trim: 1 twisted vine, 1¼" diameter x 22"

Back vines: long, flexible, twisted, gnarly vines, 1" to 1¾" diameter

Umbrella: 1 very fancy parasol

Moss (for garnish)

SUPPLIES & TOOLS

Bucksaw

Hammer and nails and/or cordless drill and decking screws

Spring clamps and bar clamps

Loppers

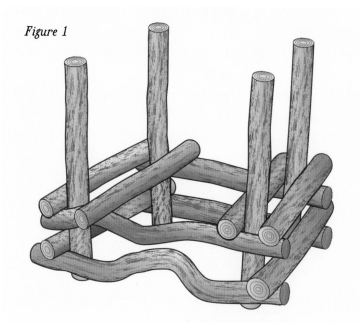

Figure 1

Note: More than any of the other adaptable projects in this book, the design of this chair must be adapted to your available building material. You may already have noticed that the specifications in the materials list quickly become somewhat sketchy. Soon after you begin building this chair, the nature of the vines will render your ruler nearly useless. We will describe the building of the chair shown in the photograph, knowing that it will be impossible to reproduce. While reading these instructions, please pay more attention to the method than to maddening specifics.

Building the Seat

1 We begin by constructing a firm foundation for the vinous fireworks to follow. Cut four fairly straight pieces of vine 15" long for the legs. Gather some likely vines for the stretchers. Laura Spector's practice, a very sound one given her design propensities, is to leave nearly every piece longer than it needs to be. She trims after the vines have been secured to the chair, but not before she knows that length won't be needed later.

2 Start connecting the legs with seat stretchers by nailing or screwing a straight or slightly concave vine even with the tops of the two front legs placed about 18" apart. Do the same on the outsides of the two back legs. For a little more style, you might want to reduce the spacing between the back legs by 2", realizing that you'll have to make up the difference with the spacing of the seat slats.

3 Stand the legs upside down, with the front and back legs about 13" apart. Select two stretchers, and attach them to the outsides of

the legs and to the seat stretchers. Then add stretchers to the front and back in the same way. These and the remaining stretchers can be more twisted than the upper pairs.

4 Add four stretchers, running front to back, to the insides and outsides of the legs, as shown in figure 1 on page 74. Secure them to the legs and the previous stretchers. Finally, add bottom stretchers to the front and back of the chair base. The bottom front stretcher may be attached anywhere below the paired stretchers. Turn the chair right side up to decide on its placement.

Figure 2

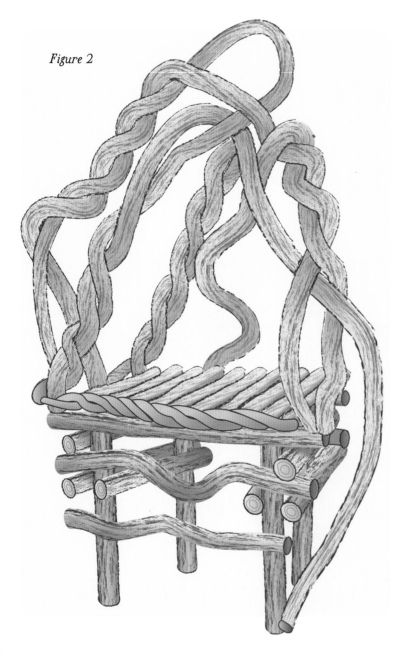

5 Add the seat slats by first laying them, front to back, on the seat stretchers so they evenly fill the space between the outside edges of the legs. When you begin nailing them in place, you can line up the back ends of the slats with the outside of the back seat stretcher, but leave the front ends long. Trace a straight line across the slats at the front of the seat, and saw them off.

6 Find a relatively straight but fancy trim piece for the front of the seat. The designer used a twisted pair of vines. Nail your trim strip to the fronts of the seat slats.

Adding the Back

7 We should probably dispense with step numbers at this point, because there's nothing linear about the rest of the process of building a chair like this one. Try to follow the courses of the vines in the photograph and in figure 2. You'll see that they're tensioned by having been woven around each other. In addition, they're attached to the base structure on the sides to brace the back and to provide more points of attachment. All you can do at this point is try different combinations of vines, holding them temporarily with clamps while you wrestle them into place. Keep trying new compositions until you find one that pleases you. If it's comfortable, too, you've hit the jackpot. Screw the vines to the seat frame and to each other to secure the whole thing in place.

8 If you have a suitable parasol, you have probably already considered its position in arranging the back vines. If you fashion a socket for the bottom end of its pole, it will be easy to remove and replace.

9 For those special occasions, a visit from the Queen Mother for instance, you might want to decorate the chair with bits of fresh moss from your rock garden. But, really, that's up to you.

HICKORY ARMCHAIR

Designed by Greg Harkins

This chair is distinguished by the composition of its back panel—sticks that weave around one another and pierce the frame on all sides. You can easily change the chair's dimensions to fit smaller and larger sitters. Or leave off the arms for a sturdy side chair.

MATERIALS

Note: All parts are peeled hickory, just like the title says, but other woods can be used for everything but the seat weaving.

Front posts: 2 limbs,
2" to 2¼"diameter x 26½"

Back posts: 2 limbs, 2" to 2¼" diameter x 46"

Side rungs: 6 branches,
1⅛" to 1¼" diameter x 19½"

Arms: 2 limbs, 2" to 2¼" diameter x 22½"

Back rungs: 3 branches,
1⅛" to 1¼" diameter x 17½"

Front rungs: 2 branches,
1⅛" to 1¼" diameter x 23½",
or one seat rung and one decorative rung

Back frames: 2 limbs, 1½" diameter x 17½"

Back panel sticks, at least 21" long

10 1"-wide hickory strips, 10' to 15' long

SUPPLIES & TOOLS

Structural epoxy

Polymerized oil finish

Saw

1" and 1¼" tenon cutters

½"-capacity electric drill with 1" and 1¼" drill bits and smaller bits for back panel sticks

Disk sander or grinder

Constructing the Side Panels

1 The chair consists of four flat panels. Since the sides are merely mirror images of each other, we'll start with them. Look at your rung stock and select four straight and smooth pieces for seat rungs. You can go ahead and cut the front posts, back posts, arms, and seat rungs to length. Use curved stock for the arms if you have it. If your posts are straight, you can cut all the side rungs, too. Otherwise, wait until step 3.

2 On the front and back posts, mark the centers of the rung mortises 6", 12", and 18" from the floor. (See figure 1 for the relative spacing of all the frame mortises.) Mark the level of the arm mortises, 26", on the back

Figure 1

posts, but don't drill them yet. With the posts held horizontal in a vise, bore 1" holes 1⅜" deep for the rung mortises.

3 Shape 1" tenons, 1¼" long, on both ends of the seat rungs. Form 1¼" tenons on the tops of the front posts and on the back ends of the arms. Fit a seat rung into its mortises, and arrange the front and back posts on your worktable so that they're parallel and their bottom ends are even. Measure between the posts at the other rung mortises to see if the distance is the same as at the seat rung. Cut the other rungs 2½" longer than the distance between the posts. Make tenons on both ends, and fit the side together.

4 Stand the side upright, and hold its arm so that its tenon pushes against the back post at the height mark you made in step 2 and it's centered atop the front post. Mark the center of the tenon on the back post so that the mortise will be aimed at the center of the post. Hold the back post in a vise or brace the side against your table, and drill a 1¼" mortise 1⅜" deep for the arm.

5 Push the arm tenon into its mortise, and mark for the front post mortise. Bore the mortise in the bottom of the arm, and make sure the whole side fits together. Complete the other side, too, remembering that it mirrors the first side.

6 Glue the sides together using structural epoxy, and clamp them if necessary. Make sure that each side remains flat by laying it on the worktable and checking to see that both posts are parallel to the table surface. Twist the side into shape if they aren't.

Joining the Sides and Finishing the Chair

7 When the glue has cured, mark the heights of the rest of the mortises on the posts. Mark on the inside of the back posts 5", 11", 17", 24", and 40" from the floor. The front post rungs are centered at 7" and 17" from the floor. If you have a decorative or wacky limb for the front rung, you may want to adjust the height of the lower front mortises.

8 To bore the mortises for the front and back rungs accurately, lay a side on your table, marks up, and prop the back post 3" higher than the front post. Now you can drill straight down, 1¼" holes for the back frame mortises and 1" holes for the rungs. Drill the mortises in the other side in the same way.

9 As with the sides, if your posts are straight, cut the rungs and back frames to length. If not, cut the seat rungs, assemble and square up the sides, and measure the rest of the rungs and

the back frames individually. If you have curved stock for the back frames, cut the tenons so that the frames provide a comfortably concave back panel. Cut tenons on both ends of the rungs and frames.

10 Now you're ready to tackle the most creative part of building this chair: filling the back panel. Connect the two sides with just the back frames and the front seat rung. Lay the chair on its back so that you can arrange likely panel sticks. One distinctive feature of this chair as Greg Harkins makes it is the way the ends of the panel sticks go right through the back frames and posts. (See figure 2.) Weaving a diagonal stick and its branch around two main vertical elements is only one of the alternatives for filling this space.

11 When your arrangement pleases you, mark the positions for the necessary mortises and their directions. Mark the sticks for length, about 1" past the posts and frames,

Figure 2

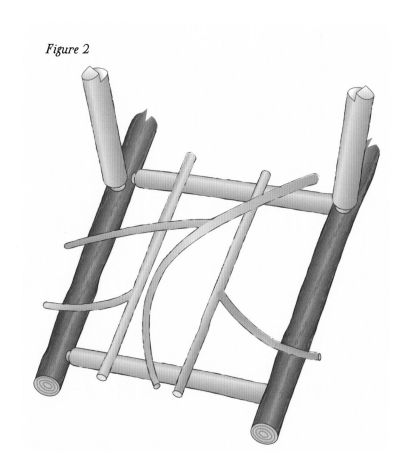

before you move them. If you can prop the whole chair far enough above the table to use a drill inside the back frame, you can leave the panel arrangement in place on the table, and use it as a reference while drilling. Drill holes just smaller than the sticks that will go through them.

12 Cut the sticks to length. You can use tenon cutters, if you have the right sizes, to reduce the ends of your panel sticks, but more likely you'll use a sharp knife to whittle them to size. Remember that your craftsmanship shows most at the exit holes, so don't reduce the diameter too much. Using a hardwood sizing gauge, as shown on page 19, would prove helpful here.

13 Dry fit the back panel to make sure everything goes together. The panel pieces usually don't need any glue, but be very sparing if you do glue them. Push the stick partway through the hole, and apply glue around the stick about 1" from the shoulder of the tenon before pushing it home. Put glue in the post mortises, and assemble the chair. Use bar clamps or web clamps if necessary, and make sure that the diagonal measurements at the seat height match.

14 Use a disc sander to round the ends of the arms, back posts, and panel sticks. If you want to use polymerized oil to finish your chair, do so now.

15 Finally, weave the seat with hickory bark strips as described by Greg Harkins on the opposite page.

Figure 3

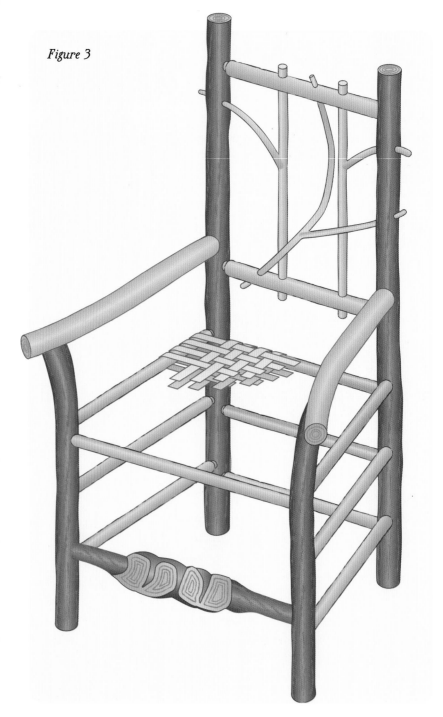

Gathering and Weaving Hickory Bark   *By Greg Harkins*

You can buy rolls of hickory bark, but to control its quality and width you must gather it yourself. Cut and peel the bark in the early spring when the sap is rising—in late spring the bark starts sticking. For an average chair seat you'll need 100' to 150' of hickory strips. They should be about ⅛" thick and ½" to 1¼" wide. The strips in one chair should all be the same width.

Peel the bark in the woods. You'll have to fell a tree upwards of 12" in diameter, so you may as well be ready to cut, cart away, and use all that wood. First, cut the tree about 1' to 2' from the ground, and remove the limbs. Use a drawknife to remove a path of the outer bark about 6" to 8" wide (depending on the tree's girth), until you get down to a cream color and the dark bark is gone. Use a hook-bill or a very sharp knife with a crooked tip. Pull the knife up the tree in a straight line, cutting through the cambium (which is about ⅛" thick) and into the wood of the tree. Try to cut strips 10' to 15' long—that's about all you can handle in weaving. Once you have several strips cut, peel them off the tree.

If you're ready to weave your seat, go ahead while the strips are fresh and wet from the tree. If you want to store your strips, lay them in the sun for three or four hours (a black asphalt driveway works well) to keep them from souring or molding. They'll still be wet and pliable, so roll them up smaller than a five-gallon bucket, and tie each bundle with sisal twine. Hang them up in the shop where air can circulate to prevent mold from growing.

Photo 1

Photo 2

Photo 3

Photo 4

To make the dried roll flexible and workable for weaving, you'll need to soak it in water. Boiling water works best (a crawfish pot on top of a wood stove is just dandy), or you can put hot water into a five-gallon bucket and let the bark soak for an hour or so, until it's pliable. Tap water is fine, too. Just let the bark soak longer—three or four hours should make it limber enough to wrap around rungs without breaking.

To weave a seat, start with the warp, wrapping strips around the front and back rungs. Use twine to tie an end to the inside of a side rung, and start wrapping from underneath the front rung (see photo 2). Leave ¼" to ½" spaces between the strips, more in the front than in the back to fill a trapezoidal seat. To join lengths of bark, just tie them together with a square knot on the bottom of the seat, as shown in photo 3. When the weaving is finished, you can untie the knots and weave the ends to secure them. When you get to the other side, tie the strip to the side rung. You can weave the ends into the bottom of the seat later.

Once you've filled the space side-to-side, start weaving the weft by weaving an end through the strips on the bottom at the back or front of the seat. Then bring the strip around a side rung and weave through the top strips (see photo 4). Push each new weft strip close to the previous strip, leaving an even space, and pull it tight again. Knot your ends on the bottom, and continue weaving. You don't need to strain the strips together, but try to keep them evenly spaced.

GARDEN BENCH

Designed by Brian Creelman

This rather ambitious project depends on suitably curved cedar for its crest rail, arms, and lower stretchers. Once you've found exciting material, though, you'll be all set to spend a couple of weekends building an impressive and comfortable bench for your garden.

SEATING: OUTDOORS OR INDOORS

MATERIALS

Back posts: 2 peeled cedar logs,
3" diameter x 33"

Back stretcher: 1 peeled cedar sapling,
1½" x 50"

Lower back rail: 1 peeled cedar sapling,
2" diameter x 50"

Crest rail: 1 naturally arched peeled cedar
sapling, 2" diameter x 47"

Back slats: 8 book-matched peeled cedar
flitches, 1½" x 3½" to 4" x 18" rough length

Front posts: 2 peeled cedar logs,
3" diameter x 24½"

Front seat stretcher: 1 peeled cedar sapling,
1¼" diameter x 53"

Front stretcher: 1 peeled curved cedar
sapling, 1¼" to 2" diameter x 53"

Side seat stretchers: 2 peeled cedar saplings,
1¼" diameter x 20

Side stretchers: 2 peeled cedar saplings,
1½" diameter x 20"

Arms: 2 book-matched, curved, peeled cedar
flitches, 2" x 7" x 26"

Seat cleat: 1 cedar plank, 1¼" x 2" x 15"

Seat slats: 5 peeled cedar flitches or planks,
1³⁄₁₆" x 3½" x 54"

SUPPLIES & TOOLS

Scrap plywood, ¾" x 6" x at least 24"

1⅝" drywall screws

Carpenter's square

2" ring-shank nails

Structural epoxy with slow hardener

Microfibers

Scrap plywood, ½" x 3½" x 20"

Scrap 2 x 4, 20" long

4" copper nails and roves, or 2" silicon bronze
screws

Polymerized oil finish (optional)

Band saw

Jointer

Power planer or hand plane

Belt sander

Bucksaw

Pruning saw

1" and 1½" tenon cutters

½" electric drill with 1" and 1½" Forstner bits

Drawknife or hatchet

Web clamps and/or bar clamps

Jigsaw

Router and 2" long ball-bearing pattern bit

Cutting the Arms and Back Panels

1 You'll be needing the back slats pretty soon, so you may as well set up to saw out the flitches for the arms and back slats at the same time. It's doubtful that you could find a sawmill to do this small (for them) job, so borrow a band saw if you don't have one, and buy a new blade for it. Get a ½" or ¾", 3 tpi, hook-tooth blade. Anything finer will clog immediately, slow down, and most likely produce wavy planks.

2 Make a jig to hold the logs in position. This can be as simple as a straight piece of plywood about 6" wide. Lay the log you want to saw on its concave side, if it has one, stand the plywood on edge next to the log, and drive two or more screws through the plywood and into the log. The screws must be short enough that they won't be in the way of the saw blade when you make the closest cut. With the plywood against the rip fence, set the fence to cut down the middle of the log, and then move it away from the blade by 2¼" for the arms and 1½" for the back slats. Saw the log, keeping the plywood firmly against the rip fence. Move the

fence in by 2¼" (1½"), and saw again. If the plywood doesn't stand vertically anymore, remove the screws, and reposition it. Then move the fence in 2¼" (1½") again, and make the last cut. This process produces two book-matched flitches from the center of each log.

3 Use a jointer to flatten the "good," or inside, faces of the flitches. Then plane them to their final thicknesses, and use a belt sander to smooth the surfaces.

Assembling the Back Panel

4 Finding the curved material for this bench is more than half the battle. The arched crest rail so dominates the design that it's worth spending some time to find a suitable sapling from which to make it. Once you've found your crest rail, cut your back posts to length, and lay them on your work surface 50" apart on center. (To make measuring easier, all dimensions between round pieces in this project will be expressed as center-to-center measurements.) Lay and prop the crest rail stock across the posts so that you can determine what part to use and whether the distance between the back posts needs adjustment. If you change the width of the back, remember to change the lengths of the front stretchers by the same amount. Mark where the insides of the posts cross the crest rail.

5 Cut the ends of the crest rail at those marks. The crest rail will have a loose tenon instead of an integral tenon as all the other frame pieces do (see figure 1). Form two 3" long tenons, 1½" in diameter, on the ends of a scrap stick. Saw the tenons from the stick. Bore a 1½" hole 1⅝" deep in each end of the crest rail, centered front-to-back and nearer the top edge of the sawn end. The two holes should be at right angles to the sawn ends, so that they would meet each other if they were extended.

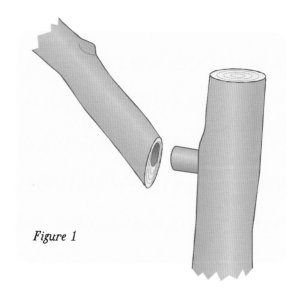

Figure 1

6 On the insides of the back posts, bore 1½" mortises 1⅝" deep, centered 28" and 21" from the floor. While the posts are in the vise, drill a 1" mortise centered 10" from the floor. Push the loose tenons into the upper post mortises, and push the crest rail onto the tenons. You may decide to cut the bottom portion of the crest rail ends at an angle to improve the appearance of their connections with the back posts.

7 Check the distance between the back posts. If it's still 50", cut the lower back rail and the back stretcher to length. Make 1½" diameter tenons on the rail and 1" tenons on the stretcher. All tenons in the bench should be 1½" long, and all the mortises are 1⅝" deep.

8 Assemble the back posts, crest rail, and lower back rail. Find the center of the lower rail and mark it. Measure out in both directions from the center, and mark the top side of the lower rail at 2¾", 8", 13¼", and 18½". Use a carpenter's square and maybe a piece of plywood held against the bottom of the lower rail to transfer those eight marks to the bottom side of the crest rail. Disassemble the back, and, with each piece in a vise, bore 1" mortises at all 16 of the marks.

9 Reassemble the back pieces. Lay the material for the back slats across the rails, centered on the mortises. Position the center pair as a book-match, and arrange each additional book-matched pair outside the previous pair. Lay a straightedge across the panels so that one of its edges is 1½" below what will be the top edge of the lower rail, where the mortises are. Draw a line across all the slats at that edge. Use a pencil to reproduce the lower edge of the crest rail across the faces of the slats. Mark the centerline of each slat from that line to the slat's upper end. Where the curved lines cross the centerline of each slat, measure upward 1½", and draw a line straight across the panel at that point.

10 Cut the slats to length at the two straight lines. Saw shoulders for the tenons a little inside the curved lines at the crest rail. Leave 1½" uncut at the center of each slat, and split off the waste from both sides. These upper ends of the slats look better if you match the outside shoulder angle on the inside of the slat, as shown in the photograph. Saw similar shoulders about 1¾" from the bottom ends of the slats. These cuts go straight into the slat. Split off the waste.

11 Form 1" tenons on all the ends of the slats. Then dry-assemble the whole back to make sure everything fits. When it does, use structural epoxy thickened with microfibers, and spread it inside the mortises to glue the back together. Start with the mortises in the crest rail, push the slat tenons in place, then add the lower back rail, and finally add the posts. Slow hardener with the epoxy resin provides enough time to assemble the whole back if you work efficiently. Use a string or rope tourniquet to hold the posts in place if you need to. Make sure that the back panel is flat by laying it face down on your work table. Then take a coffee break.

Assembling the Front Panel

12 After the back panel, the front is a piece of cake. Cut the front posts, front seat stretcher, and ornamental front stretcher to length. Make 1½" tenons, 1½" long, on the top ends of the front posts. Bore 1" mortises 11" and 17¼" from the floor on the insides of the posts. Form 1" tenons on the stretchers. Plane the top side of the seat stretcher flat, down to the level of the tenon (see figure 2). Then dry fit the stretchers and the posts. If it all looks fine, glue the front panel together, checking for flatness before you leave it. The flat side of the seat stretcher must face up. Then have another cup of coffee.

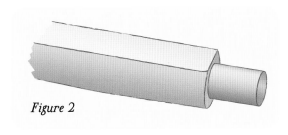

Figure 2

Adding the Side Panels

13 As you know, the side panels are mirror images of each other, so you can make both while I tell you how to make one. The side seat stretcher and the side stretcher get 1" tenons and all the 1" tenons are 1½" long, so cut the side seat and side stretchers to length, and form their tenons.

14 The side seat stretchers have a dished top surface to provide a comfy seat. The curved surface can best be formed with a router and a simple jig (see figure 3 on page 86). Draw an arc of a circle with a 40" radius on a scrap of cardboard. Mark two points 15" apart on the edge of a 3½" x 20" piece of ½" plywood or MDF. Trace the arc pattern between the two points, and cut the arc with a band saw or jig-

saw. Glue and screw the plywood to an edge of a 2 x 4 with the straight edge of the plywood flush with a face of the 2 x 4.

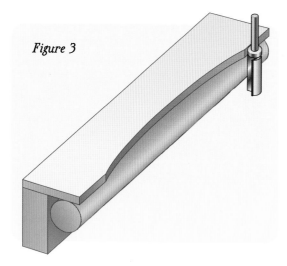

Figure 3

15 Align a side seat stretcher with the straight parts of the arched side, clamp it to the plywood, and secure it with two or three screws run through the plywood and into the stretcher. Mount the jig in a vise, and use a router with a pattern bit to form the curved surface on the seat stretcher. Remember to hide the screw holes in the seat stretchers on the inside of the bench. While you have the jig out, you can dish one face of the seat cleat as well.

16 Leave the front end of the arm long, but cut its back end straight across. Form a 1½"-long tenon on the back of the arm. To get the tenon cutter to work, you'll have to remove some of the wood on each side of the tenon at the back end of the arm. Use a drawknife or a hatchet for this job, or use a saw as you did with the back slats.

17 Mark the heights of the side seat stretcher and side stretcher mortises on the front and back posts, 8½" and 17" up from the floor. Mark the height of the arm mortise, too, 24⅛" from the floor. Lay the back and front panels on your worktable, and drill 1"

holes 1⅝" deep in the center of the posts at the stretcher mortise marks, but don't bore the arm mortises yet.

18 Dry-assemble the back and front panels and the side stretchers, and clamp the frame if necessary. Center an arm on its front post tenon with the arm tenon against the back post and pointed at its center. Mark a vertical line on the post at the center of the tenon. Drill the arm mortise 1⅜" into the back post. Push the arm tenon into its mortise. You may have to twist it a bit to get it tight. Mark the front post tenon position on the bottom of the arm. Remove the arm, and bore the mortise 1⁹⁄₁₆" deep. Be careful: you're getting pretty close to drilling right through. Repeat this process to bore the mortise for the other arm.

19 After you test the fit of the arm mortise, you can disassemble the frame and get ready for gluing. Use thickened epoxy glue spread inside the mortises. As before, add the stretchers first, then push the arms into place. Make sure the side seat stretchers have their dished surfaces up. Clamp the pieces together if necessary, and make sure that the front and back posts are parallel.

Adding the Seat

20 Sand the planks for the seat, and ease their top edges a bit. Cut four seat slats 54" long. Cut another slat to fit between the front posts on top of the front seat stretcher. Arrange the seat slats on the bench so that they have equal gaps between them. The front slat should be centered on the stretcher. Mark those positions.

21 If you know how to rivet, you can fasten the slats with copper nails and roves, as Brian Creelman does. Otherwise, use silicon bronze screws driven through pilot holes. Recess the heads slightly. After you've secured

the slats to the front and side stretchers, clamp the slat cleat, centered under the four long slats. Fasten the seat slats to the cleat, which stiffens the seat by distributing the pressure of sitting. It also prevents unwanted butt-pinches.

22 Finally, look at the front ends of the bench arms. Sit on the bench to see how the arms feel. If they need trimming,

decide on a good shape, draw it, and cut the arms with a jigsaw. Sand those ends.

23 Finish your bench with polymerized oil if you wish, following the manufacturer's directions. You can also coat the bottoms of the posts with a good layer of epoxy to protect against moisture.

Figure 4

Photo by Derek Fell

WATTLE TREE SURROUND

*I*f you have the right tree and the right yard, this surround makes a wonderful place to lounge in the shade on a summer afternoon. It's anchored with hickory or locust because of the excellent rot resistance of those species.

MATERIALS

Seat: 2 ½" exterior plywood sheets, 4' x 8'

Inner staves: 8 straight hickory or locust saplings, 2" to 2¼" diameter x 36"

Outer staves: 16 straight hickory or locust saplings, 2" to 2¼" diameter x 32"

Weavers: 75 willow branches, ¾" to 1" diameter x 6' to 7'

Seat supports: 16 willow branches, 1" to 1¼" diameter x 5½'

Seat trim: 80 willow branches, ¾" to 1" diameter x 6' to 7'

SUPPLIES & TOOLS

Dental floss

Duct tape

2½" coated nails

4" decking screws

2" decking screws

Jigsaw

Hatchet

Sledgehammer

Water level: ½" clear plastic tube, 12' long (and funnel to fit)

Bucksaw

Hammer

Lopper

Pruning shears

Cordless drill with #2 Philips driver

Note: The dimensions and instructions in this project make a surround for a 2' diameter tree and a 2' wide seat. If you wish to change these measurements, do so when laying out the plywood circle in step 1. Then follow the rest of the steps.

Laying out the Stave Circles

1 On a flat surface, butt the long edges of the plywood together. Drive a nail close to the butted edges and 48" from either end of the plywood. Use dental floss, tied in a loop around the nail and a pencil, to draw circles with 22" and 46" radii. Use dental floss because it won't stretch nearly as much as string will. Prop the plywood off the ground, and cut along both lines with a jigsaw. Don't cut up the scraps from outside the circle yet.

2 Clear a ring 4' wide around the tree, and lay the seats around the trunk. Lay the outer scraps from the plywood tight around the seat. Make a mark at eight equal intervals at the inside edge of the seat (about 17¼" each). Mark 16 points around the inside edge of the scrap so that they're the same distance from each other (about 18") and a pair of marks straddles each mark on the inside edge. See figure 1 for the relationship between the eight inner staves and the 16 outer staves.

Driving and Leveling the Staves

3 Use a hatchet to sharpen one end of all the inner and outer staves. Draw a line 12" from the pointed end to indicate ground level.

4 Push an inner stave into the ground at each mark on the plywood and just inside the seat. While standing on the seats so they don't move, use the sledgehammer to drive the inner staves 12" into the ground.

5 Remove the seat plywood, leaving the outer scraps in place. About 4" inside each mark, drive an outer stave 12" down.

6 Use a water level to mark a trimming line near the top of each stave. You'll need help from a friend for this. (Haven't you been ordering him to hold the staves while you pound away?) Mark one outer stave 17" above the ground. Fill a clear plastic tube with water, and tape one end so that it protrudes a few inches above the top of the marked stave, but don't obscure your mark. Spill small amounts of water from the tube until both ends are empty for about 6" when they're level with each other. Take the free end of the tube to the next stave, and raise or lower it until your friend tells you that the water in the taped end is even with the mark. Then mark the second stave. Repeat this friendly procedure to mark all the staves. Trim the staves straight across at the level marks.

Weaving the Outer Staves and Adding the Seat

7 Weave willow branches in and out of the outer staves from the ground to 1" from their tops. As you start each weaver, put the thicker end on the inside of a stave and nail it in place. Nail the weavers wherever necessary, and leave the narrow free ends inside the staves.

8 The seat supports connect the pairs of outer staves to their inner stave and then travel up the tree trunk. Mark a line 6" down from the top of each inner stave. Identify a pair of outer staves, and use a 4" screw to fasten the fat end of a seat support flush with the top of each stave. Then screw the seat supports to opposite sides of the inner stave just below the mark. Bend the narrow ends so that they run up the trunk. Overbending the seat supports just past the inner staves will help them stay flatter between the inner and outer circles. Install the rest of the seat supports in the same way.

9 Put the seat on the seat supports, leaving an equal overhang all around the woven circle. Use shorter screws to fasten the seat to the supports several inches from the outer and inner staves. You should be able to draw the supports up against the bottom of the seat.

Trimming the Seat

10 Now cover the seat with a layer of willow branches. Begin by nailing one course of willow trim to the outer edge of the seat. Start with a fat end and, as it gets narrow enough, add the narrow end of another willow branch next to it. Then butt a fat end to the end of the second branch. Continue in this way until you've covered the plywood edge.

11 Cover the top of the seat using the same strategy, starting at its outer edge and working inward.

12 Weave more willow branches from the seat to the tops of the inner staves in the same way as you wove the outer staves.

13 Arrange the ends of the seat supports evenly around the tree trunk, and bind them in place with willow branches nailed around them. Trim their ends even with loppers.

14 Finally, arch willow branches from each inner stave to the second stave along, tucking the ends of the branches into the weaving and securing them with nails.

Figure 1

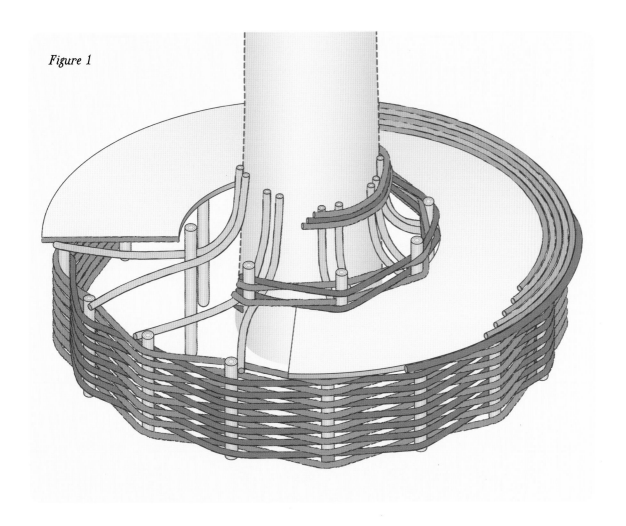

WILLOW PLANT HOLDER

Designed by Skip Davidson

This fanciful wall piece can cradle several potted plants in style. You can also form chicken wire to fit inside the basket, add sphagnum moss and dirt, and grow small flowering plants or hanging vines to make a focal point for your patio.

MATERIALS

Post and beam: 2 willow shoots, ¾" diameter x 24"

Curved pieces: 52 green willow shoots, ½" diameter x 6'

Hanger: stout cord, 12" long

SUPPLIES & TOOLS

Turpentine

Boiled linseed oil

Pruning shears

Spray bottle

Either:	**Or:**
1¼" x 18-gauge brads	1 strip of 1¼" 18-gauge brads
¾" x 18-gauge brads	4 strips of ½" 18-gauge brads
Hammer	18-gauge brad nailer
	Air compressor

Note: *"Post" and "Beam" may seem grand names for these small sticks, but these pieces anchor the rest of the structure, and the names provide a convenient shorthand for the vertical and horizontal cross-pieces, respectively. Skip Davidson uses a power nailer to fasten his willow constructions. If you don't have that equipment, you can use regular brads and a hammer. Start the brad; then hold something heavy behind the joint to make driving the rest of the brad easier. For each joint, use the longest brad that won't protrude too far. If you use a "brad gun," make sure you keep all body parts out of the line of fire.*

Assembling the Backbone

1 We'll begin building from the back. Mark the centers of the post and beam. Lay the beam on your worktable, and nail the post to the center of the beam.

2 The rest of the plant holder consists of curved pieces. Align the fat end of one shoot with the bottom end of the post, and nail it to one side of the post up to 4" above the beam. Nail another shoot to the other side of the post. Add one shoot beside each of the previous ones, nailing up to the beam. Then nail all four shoots to the beam.

3 Bend the inside shoot on each side over the outside shoot to form a loop about 10" above the beam, and nail it 4" from the end of the beam. Flip the construction over, and bring the ends of the inside shoots to the front. Trim them at the center, and nail them 6" above the bottoms of the post and sticks, maintaining a

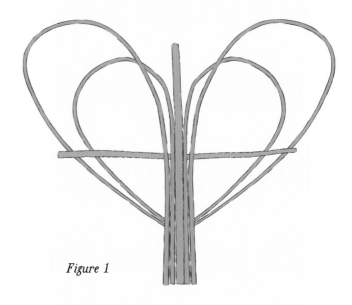

Figure 1

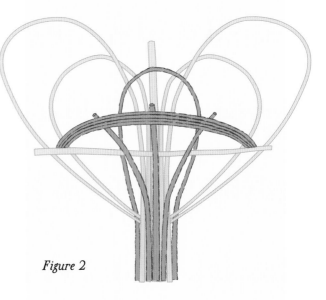

Figure 2

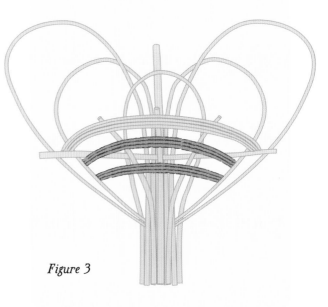

Figure 3

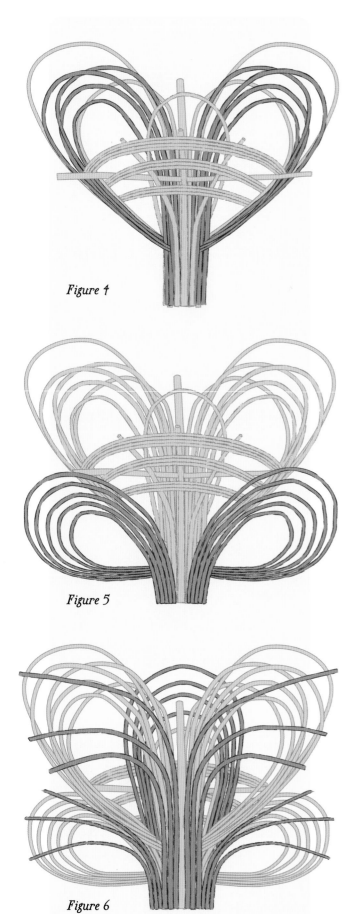

Figure 4

Figure 5

Figure 6

fair curve with the looped portion. Bend the outside shoots to form a loop 16" tall, nail them to the beam 2" from its ends, and to the backbone shoots right next to the inside shoots. (See figure 1 on page 93.)

Adding the Basket

4 On the front of the structure, align and nail the fat ends of three shoots to the post and the shoots next to it. Nail only the bottom 3" of these three shoots, and leave their tops untrimmed. Nail the end of a new shoot to the top of the beam just inside where the shorter loop on the left crosses it. Bend the shoot into a half-circle, and push the free end through on the right side of the beam next to the other short loop. Adjust the half-circle so that it protrudes 12" from the post. Nail it to the beam, and trim the excess.

5 Bend the center shoot you nailed at the bottom so that it meets the middle of the half-circle shoot, and nail them together. Divide the remaining arcs of the half-circle, and bend and nail the two outside shoots to the half-circle.

6 Add three more half-circles just inside the first at the beam and under the first at the basket ribs. Nail these to the beam and to the ribs. Trim the basket ribs just above the first half-circle.

7 Add one more loop to the back by bending a shoot into a "U" and pushing its ends down behind the beam and the large loop's thin ends. Adjust the top of this loop so that it crosses the post 3" below its top end. Nail the ends of the loop to the sides of the other loop bottom ends, and trim the ends. Turn the structure to nail the loop to the beam. (See figure 2 on page 93.)

8 Finish the basket by fastening two groups of three shoots to the fronts of the basket ribs and the insides of the short loops, as shown in figure 3 on page 93.

Adding Four More Hearts

9 On the back of the plant holder, draw a line 4" from the bottom. With their ends on the line, nail eight shoots to the back of the structure. Keep them tight together, and nail only the bottom 3" of the shoots. Begin looping the inside pair into a heart shape extending 18" above the beam. All eight

shoots cross in front of the tall and short loops from step 3, meet behind the beam between those loops, and end behind the outer basket ribs. As you work outward by pairs, shorten the heart shapes until the fourth pair matches the height of the short loops from step 3. Fasten the heart shapes to the front of the structure at their trimmed narrow ends. (See figure 4.)

Adding the Bottom Loops and Center Arches

10 Choose the narrowest 10 of your remaining shoots for the loops at the bottom of the plant holder. With their fat ends even with the bottom, nail the first pair to the fronts of the outer basket ribs. Then nail the rest of the shoots next to those ribs. The last few must be nailed to the sides of the shoots just fastened.

11 Establish the shape of the bottom loops by bending the inside shoot so that it rises to the level of the basket rim before returning to the back of the structure about 2½" from the bottom. Leave room for the other four shoots on each side to fit between the large loop end and the fat ends of the heart shapes fastened in step 9.

12 Loop, trim and fasten the rest of the loop shoots to form smaller loops inside the first. Keep the two sides symmetrical. (See figure 5.)

13 Bend four shoots into "U" shapes, and feed their ends behind the beam and over the backs of the heart shapes. Adjust the arches so that the inside one crosses at the top of the post and the rest increase in size by even increments. Trim the ends tight to the inner heart shape, and nail them to the back of the beam. (See figure 6.)

Adding Support Ribs and Finishing

14 Starting in the center of the back and aligning their bottom ends, nail the bottom 3" of six pairs of shoots to the structure and to each other. On each side, nail the inner three shoots higher, and bend them to cross the arches and hearts, as shown in figure 6. Nail them to the outer heart shoots, and trim the ends. Bend the rest of the shoots to support the bottom loops, nail them, and trim them.

15 Now go over the entire plant holder, adding brads at crossings to solidify the structure. Mix equal parts of turpentine and boiled linseed oil in a spray bottle, and saturate the plant holder. Leave it outside to dry. Finally, tie the cord around the top two supporting ribs on each side for a hanger.

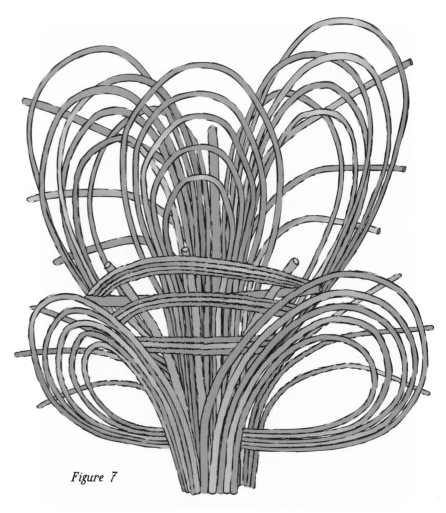

Figure 7

Designed by Joel Cole

LOG ARBOR

This majestic arbor goes together quickly once you've gathered your materials. It provides two large trellises for climbing plants and plenty of room for hanging baskets and wind chimes.

MATERIALS

Posts: 4 logs, 5" to 6" diameter x 120"

Roof beams: 2 saplings, 3½" to 4" diameter x 66"

Rails: 4 limbs, 3" diameter x 58"

Roof joists: 5 limbs, 3" diameter x 66"

Horizontal panel pieces: 6 branches, 1½" to 2" diameter x 54"

Vertical panel pieces: 6 branches, 1½" to 2" diameter x 58"

Gravel or stones

SUPPLIES & TOOLS

8 2 x 4s and stakes for bracing the posts

Lumber crayon

16d nails

8 8" TimberLok screws

30 6" TimberLok screws

24 4" TimberLok screws

18 3" TimberLok screws

Bucksaw

Post-hole digger and/or garden shovel

2 stepladders

Hammer and a maul

⅜" or larger cordless drill with hex driver

Erecting the Posts

1 Go ahead and cut all the pieces to length. You can use green wood for this project because it uses only mechanical fastenings, but drier stock may last longer. Refer to figure 1 on page 98 to see how the pieces fit together.

2 Find a dry spot for your arbor if you can, and lay out a 48" square. Centered on each corner of the square dig a hole 24" deep for a

post. Fill the bottom of each hole with 6" of gravel or stones for drainage. Find some strong and patient helpers to erect the posts, fill in around them, and brace them in vertical positions with 2 x 4s nailed to the posts and to stakes driven into the ground. You'll need two 2 x 4s at right angles to each other for each post.

Building the Roof

3 Decide which will be the open ends of your arbor, and make crayon marks on the

inside of each post 18", 72", and 96" above the ground. If your site is uneven, you may have to level the beams and rails by eye as you add them to the arbor.

4 With friends and ladders, lift a roof beam into position, centered on the top marks of two posts. The roof beams run parallel with the panels. Fasten the beam to the posts with two 8" screws at each post. Center the rails at the other marks, level them, and fasten them with two 6" screws at each crossing. Fasten the

Figure 1

remaining roof beam and rails to the other two posts.

5 Hoist a roof joist into position across the ends of the roof beams and against the outsides of two posts. Drive a 6" screw through the joist and into each post, and drive another into each beam. Install a joist at the other ends of the beams. Distribute the remaining joists between the posts, and fasten them with one 6" screw at each crossing.

Adding the Panels

6 Distribute three horizontal panel pieces between the rails on one side of the arbor, and screw them to the insides of the posts with 4" screws. Do the same on the other side with the remaining horizontal panel pieces.

7 Working on the outside of the arbor, install the vertical panel pieces, using 4" screws to fasten them to the rails. Fasten each panel crossing with a 3" screw.

8 Remove the 2 x 4 bracing, and start planting some flowering vines.

POTTING BENCH

Designed by Cheryl Evans

The branched saplings in this potting bench add visual interest and offer plenty of chances to exercise your ingenuity. While some of the branches are purely decorative, most strengthen the structure with natural connections.

MATERIALS

Back posts: 2 saplings, 1¼" to 1½" diameter x 54"

Shelf stretchers: 5 saplings, 1" diameter x 48"

Back braces: 2 saplings with branches, 1" diameter x 52"

Center brace: small branch, ¾" diameter x 28"

Back stretchers: 2 saplings with branches, 1" diameter x 48"

Front posts: 2 saplings, 1¼" to 1½" diameter x 36"

Shelf supports: 4 sticks, 1" diameter x 20"

Side braces: 2 sticks with branches, ¾" diameter x 34"

Shelves: 48 young saplings or willow shoots, ¾" diameter x 48"

Top shelf supports: 2 sapling crotches, ¾" diameter x at least 16"

SUPPLIES & TOOLS

1½" to 2½" nails

Turpentine

Boiled linseed oil

Bucksaw

Loppers

Pruning shears

Hammer

Carpenter's square

Spray bottle

Building the Back Panel

1 Cut the back posts to length, and mark them at 9", 35", and 50" from the floor.

2 Nail three shelf stretchers to the backs of the back posts. The stretchers should lie directly on the marks and extend past the posts by 2" on each end.

3 Stand the back panel on its feet to make sure the posts stand upright. When they do, lay the back panel carefully on your work surface with the back side (with the stretchers) up. Nail the back braces to the back posts, with the braces positioned diagonally between the two lower stretchers. Nail the braces together where they cross, and use any branches on the braces to strengthen the structure by nailing them to stretchers or posts.

4 Trim any excess back brace material about 1½" beyond the posts. Position the center brace parallel with the posts where the back braces cross. Then nail the center brace to the lower stretchers and the back braces.

5 Use saplings with several long branches for the back stretchers. One of these goes midway between the upper shelf stretchers, and the other sits on top of the back posts. Nail them in place, and then bend and nail their branches to form swooping lines on the back of the bench. You may want to add additional branches to fill out your design.

Adding the Front Panel

6 Nail the remaining shelf stretchers to the fronts of the front posts at the same heights as their counterparts on the back.

7 Connect the front and back panels by nailing a shelf support to the outsides of the posts right under the shelf stretchers. Leave 1"

of each end of the shelf supports overhanging the posts. Make sure that the structure looks square before nailing the supports to the stretchers, too.

8 Use branched sticks as diagonal side braces to keep the sides square. Nail them to the front and back posts as you did with the back braces.

Adding the Shelves and the Finish

9 Cut all the shelf pieces to length. Arrange the fattest ones on the supports for the bench surface to fill the space between the posts. Hold a heavy object under the shelf support while you nail the shelves to the supports.

10 Use the next largest shelf pieces to make the lower shelf, and secure it as before.

11 The top shelf supports include "grown" braces. Their branches curve down and back from near the front of the support and get nailed to the back posts. Cut the top shelf supports a few inches below where the branches start. Nail the straighter part of a support to the top of the upper shelf stretcher. The support should lie against the outside of the back post and should extend 8" in front of the post.

12 Square the top shelf support with the back post, and nail it to the post. Then bend the branch down the outside of the post, keeping the support level, and nail the branch to the post in two places. Install the

other top shelf support in the same way. (See the detail photo on page 100.)

13 Arrange the shoots for the top shelf, and nail them to the supports, using a counterweight as before.

14 If you can bear not to use the bench for a few days, you can protect it by spraying a mixture of equal parts turpentine and boiled linseed oil. Spray a second coat after the first coat has dried. Add a third coat if you wish. The finish helps keep moisture from penetrating the sticks, adding years to the life of your new bench. Still, it's wise to store the potting bench under cover and to use it on a dry, hard surface.

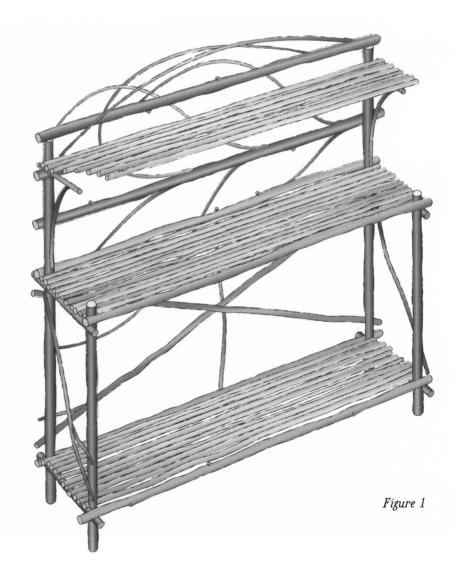

Figure 1

Rustic Furniture of the Southern Appalachians

By Lynne Poirier-Wilson

Rustic furniture was produced in the Southern Appalachians at least as early as 1847, based on a dated chair from Valley Crucis Abbey near Boone, North Carolina. Its heyday, however, came in the late 19th and early 20th centuries with the expansion of the tourist market.

Rustic furniture did not just spring from the Appalachian landscape fully formed. During the 18th century in England, a time of an intense focus on the natural, Thomas Chippendale and Robert Manwaring published examples of rustic chairs and benches in their definitive works, *The Gentleman and Cabinetmaker's Director* (1762) and *The Cabinet and Chairmaker's Real Friend and Companion* (1765), respectively. This interest in the natural moved across the sea in the early 19th century, and by the 1850s American architects extolled the virtues of rustic architecture and furnishings.

The growth of the rustic furniture trade in the Southern Appalachians is tied to the mountains themselves and to those who came to visit them. With the arrival of the train in the late 19th century, the Southern Appalachians became a tourist haven, particularly for those looking for cooler air and an escape from lowland humidity. These tourists often wanted a memento of their visit. What better than a piece of rustic furniture that bespoke the natural and the primitive feeling of the mountains? To cater to this interest in nature, many hotels and spas featured rustic fencing, bridges, railings, and outdoor seating. Photographers, commemorating mountain excursions, often used rustic background accessories. The market for rustic work was established.

With rhododendron, mountain laurel, chestnut, hickory, willow, and oak prevalent throughout the region, the materials for rustic furniture were at hand, ready to be used in their natural state and suited to the independent craftsperson. Besides, the work required only rudimentary tools—saws, clippers, penknives, hammers, and measures.

Most of the rustic furniture makers are unknown. Some were itinerant workers who moved from area to area to sell their wares or to trade them for other goods and services. Others opened their wagons or trucks at the side of the road to hawk their material to tourists driving by. Still others actually set up shops in areas frequented by tourists.

Two well-known makers were immigrants who pursued other careers first. John Hentschel (1866 to 1940) was born in Germany and emigrated in 1888. He first settled in Morristown, Tennessee, where he farmed the land. By 1920 he had moved to Western North Carolina and opened a rustic furniture shop, first in Black Mountain and later in Ridgecrest. Reverend Ben Davis (1870 to 1947), born in England, lived in Barnardsville, North Carolina, for a short time and then spent most of his life in nearby Woodfin. Davis is the most widely known rustic furniture maker in the Appalachians. As an ordained Southern Baptist circuit minister, he traveled to the many revival meetings held in the far western reaches of North Carolina, often staying at the homes of parishioners. He used the roots and branches of mountain laurel and rhododendron in his pieces, often combining them with recycled lumber from demolished buildings.

Many rustic practitioners distinguished their work with idiosyncratic decoration. Joseph Clarence Quinn (1882 to1973), born near Asheville, North Carolina, followed the tourist market, first to Hot Springs, Virginia, then on to Sweet Springs, West Virginia, finally settling in White Sulphur Springs, Virginia. His work was generally made from mountain laurel and rhododendron and was notched for decoration. John Crowe (1868 to 1954) was from Littleton, West Virginia. He, along with his son-in-law Edgar Williams, made singular plant stands from produce crates and the forks of small trees. Crowe first painted the stands a light color; when this dried he painted a coat of a darker color. Then he used rubber shoe heels he'd carved with wood grain patterns to stamp impressions in the fresh paint.

Rustic furniture comes in all shapes, sizes, and designs. Some is roughly hewn and seemingly slapped together; other pieces are delicately balanced and decorated. Some pieces are based on styles that have or had been popular for years, such as Chinese Chippendale, while others move off into new directions and become singular objects. All of these pieces are a lasting part of Appalachian folk tradition.

GARDEN GATE

Designed by Adele Mitchell

It's hard to imagine a grander entrance to your garden! The combination of straight and curved elements is designed for strength as well as beauty. The arch provides the crowning touch while supporting the posts to keep the gate halves in alignment.

MATERIALS

Arch posts: 2 logs, 5" diameter x 10'

Arches: 2 curved limbs, 3" diameter x 92"

Lower verticals: 8 saplings, 1¾" diameter x 12"

Lower stretchers: 4 saplings, 2" diameter x 39½"

Outer posts: 2 saplings, 2½" diameter x 75"

Inner posts: 2 saplings, 2½" diameter x 45"

Top brace: 2 curved branches, 2" diameter x 51"

Upper stretcher: 2 curved branches, 2" diameter x 39½"

Panel verticals: 2 saplings, 2" diameter x about 37"

Middle stretchers: 4 saplings, 1½" x 19"

Panel fill: about 12 curved branches or vines, 1" diameter x various lengths

SUPPLIES & TOOLS

3 TimberLok screws, 5"

4 TimberLok screws, 4"

Epoxy with slow hardener and microfibers

1 4' x 8' sheet of ½" plywood

Decking screws, 2½" to 4"

4 Screw hook and eye hinges

Bucksaw

Plumb bob and long spirit level

Bar clamps

Web clamps

½" electric drill

Hex driver bit for TimberLok screws

1¼", 1½", and 2" spade or Forstner bits

1¼", 1½", and 2" tenon cutters

Philips driver bits

Loppers

Blocking and shim wedges

Building the Arch

Note: Since setting the arch posts presents the biggest challenge in this project, you should begin with the arch. Once you have the arch in place, you can adjust the measurements for the gates to fit the actual opening. The length of the posts assumes foundation holes more than 2' deep, and the length of the arches assumes an 86" span between the posts.

1   Cut the arch posts to length, and lay them on the ground with their inside surfaces 86" apart. Shim them if neces- sary to put them on the same plane. Measure the diagonals to make sure the ends are even.

2   Cut the arches to length, measured in a straight line. On their ends, cut 2" tenons 3" long. The tenons must align with each other, and not along the arch pieces at their ends, so that the mortises can be bored straight into the posts.

3   Lay and prop the arches in place near the tops of the posts. The upper tenon should be about 3" from the tops. When everything looks right, clamp the arches where they touch,

and drive three 5" TimberLok screws to hold the arches together.

4 Mark the centerlines of the arch tenons on the posts, and bore 2" holes 3¼" deep.

5 Dry fit the tenons. Mix some epoxy thickened with microfibers, spread it inside the mortises, and drive the posts onto the tenons. Measure again to make sure that everything lines up correctly and remains square. Then drive a 4" TimberLok screw into the posts across each tenon to help hold it in place. Do not disturb the arch for 48 hours.

6 Dig holes deep enough to sink the posts 2' in the ground. Scrape loose soil out of the bottoms and throw in drainage gravel. Figure out how to make sure that the posts will stand on foundations level with each other. Gather staging material, and temporary supports, and lots of power, and plan carefully how to set the arch in place. Make sure that the posts stand plumb. Tamp the gravel and soil hard and often as you fill the holes, and leave your temporary supports in place as long as you can.

Building the Bottom Panel

7 Since the two sides of the gate are equivalent but not equal, we'll describe how to build one, leaving you to use the same setup to build the second. Divide the quantities of pieces in half to arrive at the correct number for each side. Measure the actual distance between the two posts you installed. If it differs from 86", you must adjust the horizontal measurements on the gates accordingly. Draw two long lines on the plywood, parallel with its edges and 41" apart. That allows 2" for the hinges and clearance between the two halves. Check your hinges to see if that seems right.

8 Cut the lower verticals to length, and cut 1¼" tenons on both ends. In this project,

all 1¼" tenons are 1½" long, and all 1½" tenons are 1¾" long. Their mortises should be bored ⅛" deeper than the tenon lengths.

9 Lay the inner and outer posts on the plywood with their bottom ends at its edge and their outsides directly above the lines. Clamp them in place.

10 Measure the distance between the posts near their bottom ends, and add 3". Cut the lower stretchers to that length, and form 1½" tenons on both ends.

11 Mark five equal portions between the shoulders on the lower stretchers (about 7¼" each) to find the centers of the mortises for the lower verticals. Bore mortises at the marks.

12 Dry fit the joints, and then glue them with epoxy. Clamp the stretchers if necessary. Make sure the ends are even by measuring their diagonals.

Adding the Top Brace and Upper Stretcher

13 Lay the lower stretcher assembly across the posts, beginning 3" from their bottom ends. Mark the centers of the tenons on the posts, and bore the mortises. While the posts are next to each other with the mortises upward, bore the mortises for the top brace, 2" from the top of each post.

14 Before you dry fit the lower stretcher assembly and the posts, bore a 1¼" mortise at the top center of the top lower stretcher. Then assemble the parts made so far. Now you must choose the material for the top braces and the upper stretchers. Arrange the pieces for both sides of the gate so that they will look good together. Notice that the design calls for two curved branches that run next to each other near the inner post. I'll wait patiently while you look. Take your time.

15 Lay the top brace across the posts above its mortises. Mark the cutting lines (in line with the posts), and mark the centerlines of the tenons (perpendicular to the posts). Clamp the top brace to the posts while you mark the upper stretcher for length.

16 Cut the brace and stretcher to length, and cut 1½" tenons on both ends of each. Pull the posts apart far enough to dry fit the brace.

17 With the upper stretcher lying across the posts, mark the center of its tenon on the inner post. The mortise in the outer post should be at, or very close to, the same distance from the bottom of the post. If it isn't, adjust the upper stretcher. When you've marked both mortises, take the gate apart enough to remove the brace and bore the new mortises.

Figure 1

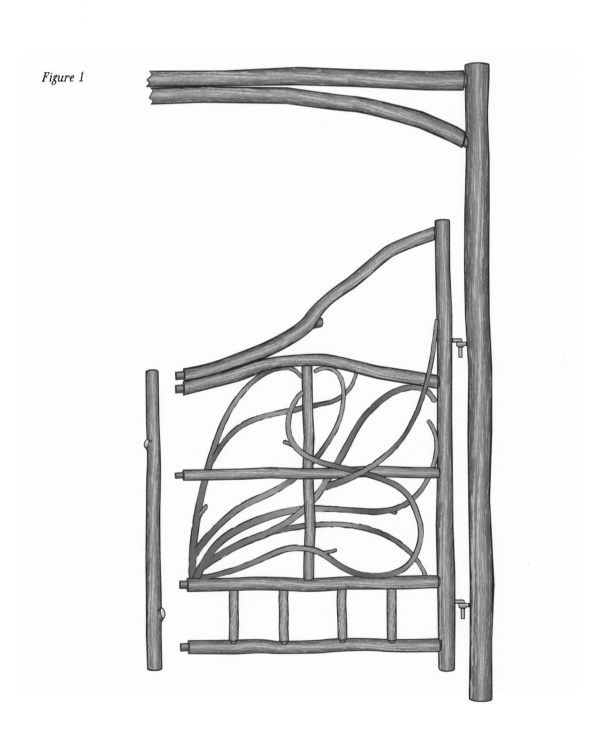

Completing the Frame

18 Reassemble the gate with the upper stretcher in place. Find a stick for the panel vertical, make sure it's long enough, and cut a 1¼" tenon on one end. Push and twist the tenon into its mortise on top of the second stretcher. Center the other end of the vertical between the posts, and mark its centerline on the upper stretcher.

19 Mark where to cut the top of the vertical, and clamp it to the stretcher. Find a stick long enough to make both of the middle stretchers, and position it a little higher than halfway between the second stretcher and the upper stretcher. Mark the centerline of the middle stretchers on the posts and the panel vertical. Without moving the stick, mark it for length, and mark it at the center of the panel vertical.

20 Cut 1¼" tenons on the ends of the middle stretcher stick. Then cut it in half at the center mark, and cut tenons only 1" long on the new ends. Cut the vertical to length and form its tenon.

21 Bore mortises for the panel vertical and the middle stretchers. The mortise in the vertical goes straight through.

22 Dry fit all the frame pieces for the gate. Then disassemble them, put epoxy in the mortises, and reassemble the frame. Clamp it together with long bar clamps or web clamps on the plywood, so that you can check its squareness and flatness.

23 Build the second side while referring to the first to make sure that the various parts line up the way they should.

Filling the Panels

24 Stand the two sides of the gate next to each other, leaning against a wall. As you choose filler pieces for the middle panel, consider both sides at once to achieve visual balance if not symmetry. Start weaving the fill around the panel vertical and the middle stretchers. The design calls for the fill to flow from the lower inner corner.

25 When you've arranged the panel fill, start trimming it to size and screwing it to whatever frame parts it touches. Try not to leave dangling ends.

Hanging the Gates

26 First, get some help, and offer prizes for those who stay until everything is done. Screw the hook parts of the hinges into the arch posts at 6" and 72" from the ground. Make sure you install them plumb with each other.

27 Put blocks about 3" high on the ground to support the inner and outer posts. Place the gates on the blocks, and shim under the posts until everything is as right as it's going to get. Make sure the gates are plumb. Mark where the eye halves of the hinges should go. Before you move the gates, decide if the hook halves are screwed far enough into the arch posts.

28 Move the gates enough to install the hinges in the outer posts. Hang the gates and adjust the hinges to make the gates work well. This may take a bit of trial and error. Remind your helpers of the treats that await them.

29 Finally, supply a means of linking the inner posts in the closed position. A loop of rope or heavy leather over the tops of the inner posts should be fine, but you may devise more elegant solutions in the future. For now, it's enough that the gates are up and look just swell.

Designed by Cheryl Evans

WATTLE SCREEN

*T*his screen would
work as well for
focusing attention on a
singular rose bush as
for hiding a garbage
can. Once you under-
stand its construction,
it's easy to adapt the
design to a size that
will suit your purpose.

MATERIALS

Arch posts: 2 willow branches, 1" to 1¼" diameter x 9'

Arch braider: 1 willow branch, ½" diameter x 4'

Crossbars: 3 willow branches or straight hardwood sticks, 1" diameter x 27"

Rods: 2 willow branches, ¾" diameter x 36"

Braces: 2 willow branches, ¾" diameter x 10"

Weavers: 54 to 68 willow branches, ½" to ⅝" diameter x 27"

Diagonal weavers: 6 hardwood sticks with branches, ½" to ¾" diameter x 36"

Lower arch: 1 willow branch, ½" diameter x 27"

Ground supports: 2 lengths of rebar, ½" diameter x 18"

SUPPLIES & TOOLS

String

1¼" to 2" coated finish nails

Copper or galvanized steel wire

Turpentine

Boiled linseed oil

Loppers

Pruning shears

Hammer

Wire cutter

Framing square

Spray bottle

Forming the Arch

1 Lay the two arch posts end to end with their skinny ends overlapping. Adjust them so that they form a line 13' long. Lay the arch braider next to the arch posts, centered lengthwise. Start at one end of the braider and braid the three sticks together for the length of the braider. Tie the ends of the braided section temporarily with string or wire.

2 Mark lines on the arch posts 6", 40", and 52" from the fat ends of each one. Notice that the designer found a stick for the lower crossbar with a branch from which she formed the lower arch. If you have something similar, install it in this step, and leave forming the arch until later. Have a hammer, nails, and the crossbars ready on your work surface. Bend the braided portion of the arch posts to make a 24"-wide arch, measured center to center. Nail a crossbar to the arch posts at the 40" marks. Nail another crossbar at the 52" marks, maintaining the 24" spacing.

3 Take a moment to make sure the bottom ends of the posts remain even with each other. Then nail the third crossbar 8" above the second. You may have to push the posts apart to get close to 24" apart, but close is close enough. Don't strain the arch too much. While you're in the area, nail the ends of the posts and braider together, and remove the lashing.

Weaving the Bottom Panel

4 Prepare to weave the bottom panel by turning the arch structure over and laying the rods 8" inside each post. They should protrude above the lower crossbar by 1". Nail them to the crossbar.

5 Weave the first two weavers in and out of the posts and rods, beginning at the 6" marks. You will need to tie the posts together at their bottom ends to keep the weavers from pushing the posts apart. Tighten the string or wire until the 24" spacing is restored. Then nail the weavers to the posts and rods, turn the screen over, and nail them on the other side.

6 Use a framing square to make sure that the posts are perpendicular to a line between their bottom ends. The bottom weaver runs underneath one of the rods. Lay a brace diagonally from that crossing to the near post, about

3" from the bottom. Nail the brace in place. Turn the screen and install the other brace.

7 Weave the remainder of the bottom panel up to the level of the lowest crossbar.

Completing the Top Panel

8 Begin with the long diagonals, sticking their lower ends into the panel weaving next to the posts, and weaving them across themselves and the upper crossbars. Notice that Cheryl Evans used branched sticks to enliven the upper panel, even finding one whose branch provided a built-in secondary arch above the top crossbar.

9 Nail the bottom ends of the long diagonals to the lower crossbar. Then add the shorter diagonals, and nail their lower ends to the crossbar or to the posts. When you have a pleasant arrangement, nail the upper ends of the diagonal weavers in place.

10 Finally, form an arch from a short willow branch, insert it into the bottom panel weaving, and nail it to the lower crossbar.

11 To protect your screen a little and to help it turn a warm dark brown color, spray it with a mixture of equal portions of turpentine and boiled linseed oil.

12 When the finish has dried, find the perfect spot for your screen, and drive two lengths of rebar into the ground, spaced so they fit against the outsides of the posts. Use wire to bind the screen to these supports, keeping its feet off the ground.

Figure 1

Woven Birdhouse

Designed by Carla Filippelli

*B*irds are sure to build their nests in this random weave birdhouse. Its decorative vines provide fine perches and add plenty of visual interest to your garden. There is no set pattern to the weaving— just let your imagination guide you.

MATERIALS

Weavers: 20 to 30 strips of thin bark or flat reeds, ½" to 1" wide x 4' to 6'

Entrance trim: 1 or 2 long lengths of #4 (2.75 mm) round reed (available at craft stores)

Vines: lengths of wild vine: grape, bittersweet, honeysuckle, wisteria, etc.

SUPPLIES & TOOLS

Scissors

Small spring clamps

Weaving the Birdhouse

1 Fashion this birdhouse using random weave, which the designer describes as "a conceptual approach to basketry with no set rules or patterns." Soak your weaving materials in warm water until they're pliable. Begin by making a circle of bark or reed of a size that would fit around a cantaloupe. Shift the weaver so that it goes off at an angle, describing a new circle. Keep going until you can weave the reed in and out of existing circles. Use small spring clamps to help hold things in place during the early going.

2 When you've used the first weaver, start another by tucking it into the developing sphere. Keep one hole, about 1¼" to 1½" in diameter, open to the interior. Use various materials and sizes of weavers as the spirit moves you, elaborating and filling the sphere.

3 Once your house is closed in, use round reed to stitch around the entrance hole, making a tight and sturdy circle. Loop the reed around any adjacent weavers as you go round and round the entrance. Tuck the stray ends back into the weaving.

Decorating and Hanging the Birdhouse

4 Finally, decorate the house with wild vines, snaking them out and around the weavers or adding flat reed to hold a section of vine. Use enough vines to partially camouflage the birdhouse. Remember to weave the vines firmly enough to support a curious bird.

5 Decide on a well-supported vine from which to hang the house, and find a site free of preying cats.

SKY-HIGH BIRDFEEDER

Designed by Greg Ani

As a model of a rustic pavilion, this jaunty structure could be considered a postmodern work of art…or a dandy bird feeder.

MATERIALS

Legs: 4 birch saplings,
1¼" to 2" diameter x 64"

Floor: ¾" exterior plywood, 9" x 11"

Cross braces: 2 birch sticks,
¾" to 1" diameter x at least 16"

Corner posts: 4 willow shoots,
⅝" to ¾" diameter x 9"

Short walls: 10 willow shoots,
½" diameter x 9"

Long walls: 10 willow shoots,
½" diameter x 12"

Short perches: 2 willow shoots,
½" diameter x 16"

Long perches: 2 willow shoots,
½" diameter x 18"

Roof supports: 2 willow shoots,
½" diameter x 17"

Gables: 2 ⅜" exterior plywood, 3" x 16"

Gable logs: willow shoots,
½" diameter, to cover gables

Roof: 2 ⅜" exterior plywood, 8⅝" x 17"

Peak log: 1 willow shoot, ½" diameter x 19"

Roof logs: 72 willow shoots, ½" diameter x 9"

SUPPLIES & TOOLS

Epoxy resin with slow hardener and
microfibers

Scrap wood or plywood for braces

¾" and 1" brads

2" nails

2" decking screws

4 lengths of 1½" ID plastic pipe, 9" long

Bucksaw

Web clamp or heavy twine

Loppers

Pruning shears

Hammer

1" and ⅝" tenon cutters

Drill with 1" and ⅝" bits

Handsaw or jigsaw

Note: These instructions explain how to make a birdfeeder with a willow-faced roof and gable. The feeders in the photo have a simpler, varnished-plywood design with willow shoots on the edges to hide the plies. If you want to make the feeder in the photo, follow the steps here, but omit the willow covering. Then add a bit of decoration to the gable ends. We've specified diameters of willow shoots in the materials list, but anything close will work just fine. You'll be able to use more of the shoots you gather if you can cut several pieces from each one.

Making the Base

1 Cut the legs to length, and form 1" tenons ¾" long on their top ends.

2 On the plywood floor, mark centers for mortises ¾" in from the sides at each corner, and drill 1" mortises right through.

3 Dry fit the legs and the floor. Stand the legs and floor upright, and move the bottoms of the legs outward until you have a small amount of splay.

Figure 1

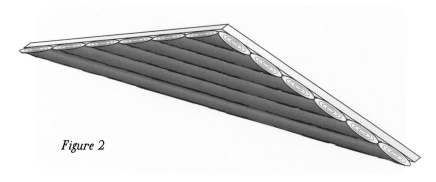

Figure 2

4 Cut ⅝" mortises in the legs, centered 7" from the floor on one diagonal pair and 8" from the floor on the other pair. Hold a cross brace against a diagonal pair of legs to mark its length, and cut tenons on both ends of the brace. Do the same with the other brace, measuring it against the remaining legs.

5 Loosen the legs enough to dry fit the cross braces. If they fit, go ahead and glue them to the legs, spreading epoxy thickened with microfibers in the mortises before pushing the tenons home. Use a web clamp or twine to hold the joints together.

6 Nail lengths of scrap lumber or plywood near the tops of the legs as temporary braces, and remove the floor by knocking it upward.

Building the House

7 Cut the posts to length, making sure to cut their bottom ends square across. With the posts and floor upside down, drive one nail through the floor and into the end of each post. Align the posts flush with the corners of the floor, as shown in figure 1 on page 115.

8 Cut the short walls to length and nail them in place, beginning at the bottom edge of the floor. Work with the two end posts hung on the edge of your bench so that you can easily nail the walls to the posts. Keep the walls tight and parallel with the floor.

9 Cut the long walls to length, and nail them as you did the short walls. Then add the long perches to the tops of the long walls. The short perches rest across the ends of the long perches. Nail them to the posts and to the long perches.

10 Nail the roof supports to the posts, centering them 7¾" above the floor.

Raising the Roof

11 Mark the slope of the gables by drawing lines from the center of one long edge of the plywood to each of the corners on the opposite edge. Cut out the gables with a handsaw or jigsaw.

12 Cover the outside of each gable with willow shoots. Nail the shoots in place, letting them overhang the angled edges. When the gable is covered, turn the gable over, and use the plywood edge as a guide to trim the ends of the shoots flush with the gable. (See figure 2.)

13 Cut out the plywood roof pieces. The gable ends fit just outside the posts, so measure that distance and transfer it to the undersides of the roof pieces. Draw lines at

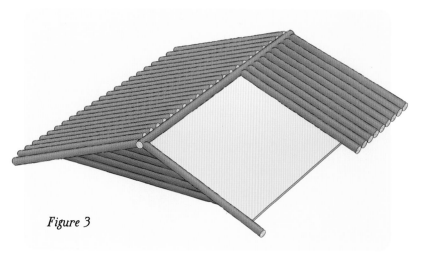

Figure 3

your marks to indicate the inside of the gable ends. Nail the roof pieces to the gables, making the roof pieces meet at the peaks of the gables.

14 Fasten the peak log along the crevice made by the roofs, nailing through the peak into the edges of both roofs.

15 Cut enough shoots to cover the roof. Begin by nailing four shoots to the roof end edges so that they abut the peak, as shown in figure 3. Nail the roof logs in place, choosing and arranging them to cover the whole roof.

16 Rest the roof structure on the roof supports, straddling the posts. Reach inside to nail the posts to the gables. Then nail through the roof supports at an angle into the gables.

Finishing the Feeder

17 Before removing the temporary braces from the legs, run a screw up through the intersection of the cross braces. Then cut 2" long tenons on the bottoms of the legs, as shown in figure 4. These tenons should end up being vertical, and should fit easily into the 1½" plastic pipe.

18 Spread epoxy into the mortises in the floor, and push the feeder onto the legs. Let the glue cure before you remove the temporary braces.

19 When you have found a good spot for your feeder, use the leg tenons to mark positions for the pipe anchors. Drive the plastic pipes as far into the ground as they will go. You may have to trim them with a handsaw to level the feeder. Push the legs into the pipes. You may want to anchor the feeder even more by running screws through the pipe walls into the tenons.

20 Fill the feeder with birdseed, and stand back.

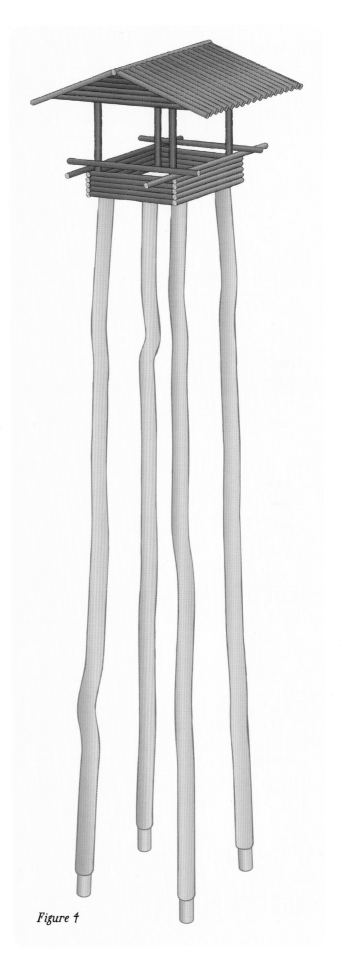

Figure 4

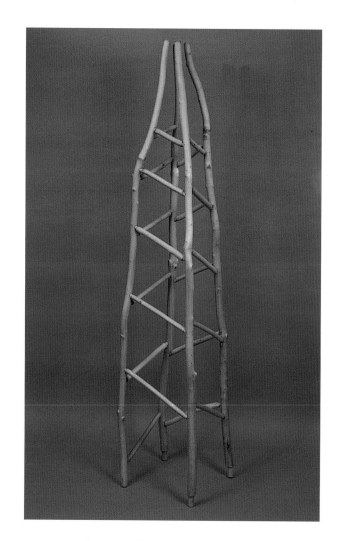

Designed by Paul Ruhlmann

PEELED-POLE TRELLIS AND OBELISK

If you have just a little time, make a rustic ladder trellis to give your climbers a leg up. If you have a little more time, add three sides for an obelisk that will stand up and be noticed in your garden.

MATERIALS

Posts: 4 peeled limbs, 1½" diameter x 6' to 7'

Rungs: 21 peeled sticks, ¾" to 1" diameter, various lengths

Ornament for the top

SUPPLIES & TOOLS

Large rubber band or string

Epoxy with slow hardener and microfibers

Galvanized finishing nails or decking screws

Paint or polymerized tung oil

Vise

Knife

Small saw

Drill with ⅝" bit

⅝" tenon cutter

Note: To make a ladder trellis, follow the instructions for making the first side of the obelisk, but lay out the posts with 6" between them at the top.

Making the First Two Ladders

1 Lay two of the posts on your work surface with their fatter, bottom ends about 18" apart and the top ends close together, maybe 1" apart, depending on the ornament you choose. The ornament connects, and is held by, the tops of the posts. It can be a turning, a square piece of wood, an interesting limb, or a found object. It will be secured with screws.

2 Lay five rung sticks at a constant angle across the posts, distributing them evenly between the top and the bottom of the ladder. Reach under the rungs to mark the centers of the mortises on the insides of the posts. Trace the rungs on the posts with the pencil to indicate the correct angle for the mortises. Measure from the insides of the posts, and mark the

rungs 2¼" out on each end. Use a small saw to cut the rungs at these marks so that they come out 4½" longer than their spaces between the posts. Lay the rungs aside in order.

3 Wrap a post with a soft cloth to protect it, and snug it in a vise with the mortise marks facing up. Tilt the post so that the traced marks run vertically. Tighten the vise, and use a sharp ⅝" bit to drill vertical holes right through the posts at your mortise marks. Ease the pressure as you get to the other side, and hold a small block of softwood against the post to minimize splitting out. Repeat the procedure with the other post.

4 Clamp a rung horizontally in the vise. If your tenon cutter has a depth gauge, set it so that the straight part of the tenon will be 2¼" long. Use the level on the tenon cutter (if it has one) to help it start straight into the rung. Push on your drill with controlled firmness to cut the tenon. Cut 2¼" tenons on both ends of all the rungs.

5 Assemble the ladder without glue. Even if the joints don't quite line up, the wood's flexibility will let you push the posts onto the tenons. Round the ends of the tenons with a knife or sandpaper. If you're making a ladder trellis, you can glue it now as described in step 9, then proceed to step 11. For

Figure 1

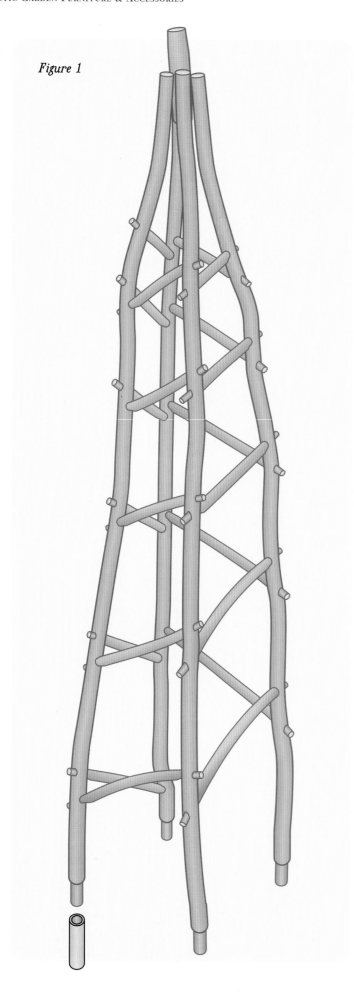

the more intrepid (or foolhardy), or those who found making the first ladder just too much fun to stop, march on!

6 Make another ladder with the other two posts. While you're laying out the spacing of the posts, check the fit of your top ornament, using the first ladder with the two new posts.

Connecting the Ladders

7 Lay the two ladders on edge with the ornament nestled in their top ends, and hold the tops together with large rubber bands or string. Now you can lay out and mark a third set of rungs between the two ladders. To drill the mortises, prop one end of a ladder to make the traced lines run vertically. Drill the mortises as before, and cut the rungs and their tenons.

8 Dry fit the new rungs to hold the first two ladders while you mark the fourth set of rungs. When the last of the mortises and tenons have been cut, loosen the third set of rungs enough to dry fit the fourth set. Don't worry if one of the posts won't touch the ground, but remember to mark the tenons before you take the obelisk apart, so that you can put it back together in the same way.

9 Use a slow-setting epoxy to glue the obelisk. Usually, we put glue in the mortises and hope it "mushes" into every area of the joint. If you do that here, most of the glue will be pushed out by the tenon, so apply epoxy, slightly thickened with microfibers, to the tenons just inside the area that will protrude from the posts. This way, the glue will have a chance to squeeze through the mortise as you push the joint together. Have plenty of paper towels handy to wipe up excess glue. If any of the joints want to come apart, use a web clamp or a string tourniquet to hold them together.

Finishing the Obelisk

10 After the epoxy has cured overnight, put the top ornament in place, and secure it with galvanized finishing nails or decking screws. Clean up any remaining marks on the posts and rungs. Stand the obelisk on a flat surface, and put spacers under the posts where necessary to make it stand straight. Find another spacer the height of tallest stack of shims, and use that with a pencil set on top to trace around all of the posts. Trim the bottoms of the posts at your lines.

11 To protect your obelisk from ground moisture, cut tenons for pipes as described on page 26. You can use a clear finish such as polymerized tung oil or, for more protection and color, paint it. See Painting and Finishing Outdoor Furniture at right for more guidance.

Painting and Finishing Outdoor Furniture
By Paul Ruhlmann

I use either milk paint or water-based acrylic paint on my outdoor pieces. Outdoor rustic furniture with the bark on is susceptible to insect damage and decay. Painted surfaces provide protection for the wood and allow for a variety of visual effects.

For centuries paint was mixed at home, using recipes that featured curdled milk, lime, and pigment as the main ingredients. This nontoxic paint, which gives an attractive flat surface, is now commercially available. If you can't find it at your local paint or craft store, check the source list at the Lark Books Web site (www.lark-books.com). I like the fact that the colors in milk paint tend to mute and soften over time, and I find this natural paint is especially nice for birdhouses.

Water-based acrylic paints also work well for outdoor pieces. On the Stone Top Bench (page 71), I first applied an acrylic base coat. I then applied spirals of painted dots using a glue syringe filled with artists' acrylic. Australian Aboriginal art inspired me to design these painted dot spirals. To arrange the dots in a smooth line, I wind a piece of string in a helical pattern around the piece. I then begin to apply rows of dots on either side of the string. There are numerous interesting effects you can achieve with painted surfaces. Michael Hosaluk has written an outstanding book on this subject called *Scratching the Surface*. Don't be afraid to experiment with many techniques and materials. You can use masking tape and stencils to help control the paint, but be sure to plan your pattern in advance on the pieces you'll be painting, so that you end up with a strong effect.

DIAMOND ROSE TRELLIS

Designed by Susan Churchill

This trellis goes together quickly to provide near-instant support to all your climbing plants. You can change the dimensions easily to fit a wide variety of locations.

MATERIALS

Posts: 2 saplings, 1½" diameter x 78"

Frames: 2 saplings, 1¼" to 1½" diameter x 48"

Long panels: 2 saplings, 1" diameter x 54"

Medium panels: 4 saplings, 1" diameter x 48"

Short panels: 4 saplings, 1" diameter x 24"

SUPPLIES & TOOLS

2½" and 1⅝" decking screws

2 9" lengths of 1" or 1½" ID PVC pipe (optional)

Cordless drill with screwdriver bit

Saw

Building the Trellis

1 Cut the posts to length. Mark lines on the posts 18" and 66" from their bottoms.

2 Cut the frames to length. Lay the posts on the ground with their ends even and about 44" apart. Lay the frames on your marks, and adjust the post spacing so that about ½" of the frames extends past the posts. Screw the frames to the posts at each crossing.

3 Lay one of the long panels across the frames diagonally, so that it lies above the frame/post crossings. Divide the excess length evenly on the two ends of the panel, and don't trim it yet. Screw the long panel to the frames.

4 Divide the length of the frames and the distance on the posts between the frames into three equal parts (about 16" each), and mark the frames and posts at the division lines.

5 Lay two medium panels parallel with the long panel, crossing the posts and frames at the pairs of marks nearer the long panel. Screw the medium panels in place.

6 Lay two short panels parallel to the others at the remaining marks, and screw them down, too.

7 Repeat the process to add the remaining panels on the opposite diagonal to the first set. You'll have to press down on the ends of these panels while you drive the screws to put the panel ends in touch with the crossing sticks below.

Finishing and Installing the Trellis

8 Drive a shorter screw into each crossing of two panel pieces.

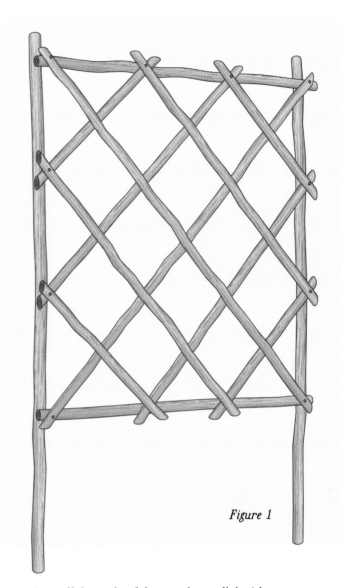

Figure 1

9 Saw off the ends of the panels parallel with the posts or frames, leaving about ½" overhanging those pieces.

10 Of course you can simply lean your trellis against a wall or fence near your climbing roses. For a little added security, screw the tops of the posts to the wall. If you want to add years to the life of the trellis, drive lengths of pipe into the ground where you want the posts to land. Whittle enough of the posts so that they fit into the pipes, and push them home. This keeps the feet of the posts from getting wet and encouraging rot. You can drive a screw through each pipe if you're worried about the trellis flying away. The mounting pipes also offer a way of supporting the trellis without a wall to lean on.

SWING ARBOR

Designed by Brian Creelman

Clearly, this is a challenging project. Just as clearly, the result is worth the effort. If you're looking for some heavy rustic construction, go to it! You don't have to be told about the satisfaction you'll find.

MATERIALS

Note: All materials are peeled cedar unless otherwise noted. As always, avoid cutting parts to length until you have to, because lengths often depend on the shapes of adjacent parts.

For Side Panels:

Posts: 4 logs, 4" to 5" diameter x 76"

Side rails: 6 saplings, 2" to 3" diameter x 38"

Side spindles: 20 branches, 1" to 1½" diameter x 23"

Upper spindles: 2 branches, 1½" diameter x 44"

Lattice: 48 green branches, ¾" diameter x 23"

For Back Panel:

Top and bottom rails: 2 saplings, 2" to 3" diameter x 72"

Truss rail: curved sapling, 2" to 3" diameter x 72"

Back spindles: 16 branches, 1½" diameter x 25"

For Roof:

Purlins: 2 logs, 3½" to 4" diameter x 96"

Collar ties: 3 logs, 3" to 3½" diameter x 38"

Rafters: 10 logs, 3" to 3½" diameter x 32"

Rafter spindles (optional): 10 log pieces, 2" diameter x 6"

Battens: 12 cedar or pine planks, 1 x 3 x 8'

Cedar Shingles: to cover 48 square feet

For Bench:

Back posts: 2 saplings, 3" diameter x 26"

Front posts: 2 saplings, 3" diameter x 16"

Arms: 2 split branches, 4" wide x 22"

Rungs: 4 branches, 2" to 2½" diameter x 20"

Seat/back rails: 4 branches, 2½" diameter x 56"

Suspension rails: 2 saplings, 3" to 3½" diameter x 62"

Seat slats: 5 cedar flitches, ¾" x 3½" to 4" x 60"

Back slats: 12 cedar flitches, ¾" x 3½" to 4" x 24"

SUPPLIES & TOOLS

Epoxy with slow hardener and microfibers

Exterior woodworker's glue

1¼" and 2" copper ring nails

4 ⅜" x 5" ring screws

24' galvanized steel chain

2 ⅜" x 5" hook bolts, with washers and nuts

10 3½" TimberLok screws

20 6" TimberLok screws if you omit rafter spindles

2 sheets of ½" or ¾" plywood, 4' x 8'

Several 4" and 5" squares of ½" plywood for end blocks

Optional anchoring method:

4 4" sonotubes, longer than your frost depth

4 ½" galvanized threaded rods, 12" long

4 ½" washers and nuts

⅝" and 2" drill bits

Bucksaw

½", 1", and 1½" tenon cutters

½", 1", and 1½" Forstner or spade bits

½" electric drill

Trimming saw

Framing square

Adjustable bevel

Hand plane or jointer

Chop saw

Hex driver for TimberLok screws

A note about layout and construction techniques: Since the members of this arbor are large and of varying sizes, we'll use center-to-center dimensions. For instance, "lay two posts 36" apart" means that the center axes of the posts will be 36" from each other. To make the measuring and joint-making easier, use Creelman's end block system described on page 18. Lines squared across the blocks at their centers provide points of reference for measuring, and the edges of the blocks help keep your mortises aligned.

One more thing: all 1½" tenons in this project are 2" long. All 1" tenons are 1½" long. All ½" tenons are ¾" long.

Making the Side Panels

1 We'll describe the construction of one side panel, and then you can go ahead and make its mirror image. As the photo shows, you can make effective use of trees cut close to the ground for the posts. Cut two posts to length.

2 Draw two lengthwise lines, 36" apart, on a sheet of plywood. Install 5" end blocks on the posts, and align them with the layout lines. On the insides of the posts, mark centers for mortises 8", 30", and 72" from the bottom ends. Bore 1½" mortises at those points.

3 To save a little heavy lifting later, turn the back post 90° to mark the mortises for the back rails. Remember to turn the back post in the opposite direction when making the second side panel. Mark centers 10½", 44", and 69½" from the bottom end block, and bore 1½" mortises.

4 Lay the posts back in position on the plywood. Measure between each pair of mortises to find the length of each of the three side rails. As always, remember to add the lengths of the tenons. Cut the side rails to length, and install 4" end blocks on the two lower rails.

5 Determine the spacing of the 10 side spindles, mark for the mortises on the two lower rails, and cut 1" mortises at the marks. Then remove the end blocks, and cut 1½" tenons on the ends of all three rails.

6 Assemble the posts and rails on the plywood to check that you've maintained the proper spacing between the posts. Twist the lower rails so that their mortises face each other. Measure for the spindle lengths, cut them to length, and cut their tenons.

7 Take the frame apart enough to dry fit the spindles. If everything works, find a branch for the upper spindle. This piece can be quite curvy, but make sure you have another branch with similar curves. Lay the upper spindle stock across the side rails, and decide where it should go. Mark for the mortises on the rails, and mark the spindle for length. Bore the mortises, trim the spindle, and tenon its ends.

8 Dry fit the side panel once more. Once everything fits, take it all apart, spread epoxy thickened with microfibers inside the mortises, and reassemble the whole side on the plywood. Make sure that the plywood is flat and that all the end blocks rest on the plywood. Use clamps, if necessary, to flatten the side panel.

9 Once the epoxy has cured, you can add the lattice branches. These should be green and pliable, so that you can bend them into position and into their mortises. Begin by marking mortise locations on both sides of the upper spindle. Starting at the middle rail, mark every 3" until you get within 6" of the top rail. If you want to add another branch running from the middle rail to the post, as shown in figure 1, mark its location and drill the mortises before adding the lowest branch to the upper spindle.

10 Bend a lattice branch to a pleasing curve, and draw the angle at which it crosses the spindle on its front. If your spindle is straight, you can use an adjustable bevel to repeatedly drill at the same angle. Curvy spindles require that you fit each lattice separately. Drill a ½" mortise at the angle you marked on each side of the spindle.

11 Cut a tenon on one end of all the lattice branches. Push the tenon into one of the bottom mortises, and bend it to the curve you had before. Mark its centerline on the post, and mark its trimming line ¾" beyond the post's near edge.

12 Trim and tenon the other end of the lattice, and bore the mortise in the post. Again push the first tenon into the spindle mortise, and gently over-bend the lattice until it pops into the mortise in the post. If that procedure didn't work too well, adjust the length of the lattice or the diameter of the mortise and/or the tenon. When you successfully dry fit several lattices in a row, you can skip that step and go right to gluing.

13 To install the lattice between the middle rail and the post, leave the first lattice in place while you bend another stick and mark its mortises. Drill both mortises, but put the first lattice in place again while you mark the length of the bottom lattice.

14 When you've completed steps 11 through 13 on one side, fit the matching lattices on the other side. Then apply exterior woodworker's glue to the mortises for each lattice in turn, and push them home.

15 Continue working up the spindle, mortising, trimming, tenoning, and gluing each lattice branch in turn. If you see that you will have trouble drilling the mortises for the last lattices, avoid gluing any pieces that will get in your way.

16 Build the other side in the same way, remembering to cut the mortises for the back rails on the opposite side of its back post.

Building the Back Panel

17 To lay out the back panel, you'll need a flat area about 4' x 7' on which you can draw. One way is to tack the long edges of two sheets of plywood together using scrap plywood nailed near the ends of the abutting edges. Draw two parallel lines, perpendicular to one edge and 72" apart, across the plywood surface.

Figure 1

18 Stand your side panels on edge, back posts down, and align their centers with the layout lines. The end blocks should keep the sides upright. Measure for the lengths of the three back rails.

19 The design depends on a truss rail with a good curve, so search for a worthy tree. Cut the back rails to length, measuring in a straight line between the ends of the truss rail.

20 Then cut tenons on the three rails. The truss rail tenons must be perpendicular to the posts. If you're having trouble cutting them on the truss rail itself, you can cut it to the distance between the posts and cut mortises in its ends. In this case, use slip tenons, 4" long, made from another branch.

Figure 2

Completing the Side Panels

24 Now you can remove the end blocks from the posts. Cut 1½" tenons on the tops of the posts.

25 This is a good time to decide whether to anchor your swing arbor, because it's easy to get at the bottoms of the posts. To prepare the posts for anchors, drill a ⅝" hole 6½" long into the bottom of each post, using the screw hole as a center.

26 Measure 5½" up the inside of each post (the back of a front post, for instance), and drill a 1½" hole about 1" past the first hole. The ⅝" hole will accept a ½" threaded rod, and the 2" hole provides room to install a washer and nut.

Making the Roof Frame

27 To build the roof, you'll need at least 7' of headroom. Assemble the back and side panels in their normal, upright position. Check to make sure that the centers of the tenons on the back posts are still 72" apart. Cut the purlins to length, and install end blocks. Mark the purlins for the post mortises, 72" apart and equidistant from the ends of the purlins. Roll the purlins 90° in opposite directions, and mark the locations of the collar ties, one in the center and one 32" in each direction. Bore all those holes with a 1½" bit.

28 Tap the purlins in place on the post tenons. Measure for each collar tie, cut it to length, and cut tenons on both ends. Dry fit and glue the collar ties using epoxy, but don't

21 Push the back rails and the truss rail into their mortises in the back posts, and make sure the posts are still 72" apart. Lay out the mortises for the back spindles, spacing them equally between the posts, as shown in figure 2. Cut 1" mortises at your marks. You may be able to bore those holes with the rails in place. If you take them out of the posts, reassemble the back for the next step.

22 Measure the distance between each pair of mortises, add 3" for the tenons, cut the spindles to length, and tenon both ends.

23 Dry fit the complete truss panel with the rail tenons in the posts. Then take the back panel apart, and glue it together. Don't glue the back panel to the posts yet, but push the posts onto the rail tenons to hold the truss panel while the glue cures.

glue the purlins to the posts. When the glue has cured, move the purlin assembly to a comfortable working height.

29 Prepare the rafters by planing a flat surface about 2" wide on each one, as shown in figure 3. This provides a reference surface for cutting their joints and aligning them above the purlins.

30 Cut one end of each rafter at 22.5° on your chop saw, holding its flat surface against the fence. Assemble five pairs of rafters by driving two or three 3½" screws across the joining surfaces you just cut. Make sure that the flat surfaces line up and the angles made by the pairs are all the same.

Now you have a decision to make. The photograph shows the rafters supported by short spindles above the purlins, but the drawings show the rafters nestled directly on the purlins. The rafters must all be at the same height so the roof lays flat. Brian Creelman likes to adjust the rafter heights by adjusting the lengths of those spindles, but you can cut shallow notches in the purlins and adjust the rafter heights by changing the depth of the notches. It's your choice, given your proclivities. I'll assume that you can figure out how to pursue the notch

method and just describe here how to install the rafter spindles.

31 Near the center of one long edge of your plywood, draw a perpendicular line, and mark it 12½" from the edge. Mark points 30" either side of that line at the edge of the plywood. Draw lines between those points and the 12½" mark, and draw lines parallel with the centerline and 18" either side of it. Lay a rafter pair on the drawing so that its peak is on the centerline and the rafters follow the slanted lines. Use a square held vertically to mark a mortise directly above each of those last two lines.

32 Clamp the rafters to the plywood, and bore 1½" mortises at the marks and aligned with the layout lines. Repeat this process to cut mortises in the other four pairs.

33 Mark and cut 1½" mortises in the tops of the purlins. One goes at the center and two more on each side on 22½" centers.

34 Trim the rafter spindles to length, and cut mortises on both ends.

35 Push a spindle into each mortise in the purlins, and mount the rafters on the

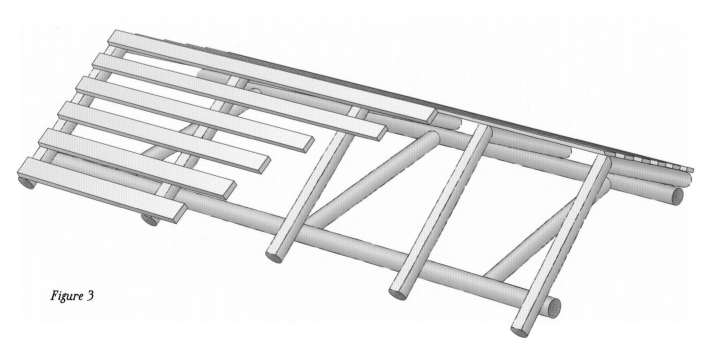

Figure 3

spindles. Use a long straightedge to find out which spindles need shortening and by how much. Change their lengths accordingly, and lengthen the tenons, and try again until you have both sides of the roof flat across.

36 Go ahead and glue all those joints together. You can tack a batten or two across the rafters to keep them vertical.

Anchoring and Assembling the Arbor and Finishing the Roof

37 It's time to put the arbor together, but you don't want to carry the whole thing very far. You probably know where it's going by now, so prepare the site. Keep the posts out of the dirt, and provide good drainage so they don't stand in water, either. To keep the arbor from moving when you swing, or in a heavy wind, make a plywood pattern for the threaded rods that will connect the posts to the concrete footers. If your measurements have adhered to those given, drill a ½" hole centered at each corner of a 3' x 6' rectangle.

38 Dig holes for the sonotubes deeper than your frost line. Level the tops of the tubes, back-fill their holes, and fill them with concrete. Position your pattern so that the holes come as close to the centers of the sono-tubes as possible. Push a threaded rod into each hole, keeping it vertical, until 5" remains above the plywood. Run a washer and nut right down to the plywood to keep the rod in position.

39 When the concrete has cured, glue and assemble the truss panel, lower back rail, and the sides. Do this as close as possible to the footings. Remember to remove the washers and nuts from the threaded rods. It will take at least three people to move the arbor over the rods, and you should do so as soon as you assemble the frame. Make sure everything is plumb, and reach into the access holes in the

sides of the posts to install the washers and nuts. You can whittle plugs for these holes, or cut plugs with a tenon cutter. Don't glue the plugs in place, but leave them a bit proud of the posts in case you need to adjust the nuts.

40 While your helpers are still available, lift the roof frame into place after gluing the insides of the purlin mortises.

41 Nail skip-sheathing battens to the rafters at the spacing your single exposure shingles require. Then proceed with installing the shingles.

Making the Bench

42 Construct the bench in the same way as the arbor: two side panels connected with four rails. Cut the front and back posts to length, and install 4" square end blocks.

43 Label the end blocks as to front and back, left and right, and top and bottom, and add arrows pointing to the two sides that will get mortises. All the tenons in the bench will be 1½" diameter x 1¼" long. Mark the side rung mortises first, 3½" and 8" above the bottom end blocks. Turn to the insides of the front posts, and mark the seat rail mortise at 8". On the insides of the back posts, mark for mortises at 8", 12", and 24" from their bottom ends. And on the fronts of the back posts, the arm mortises are 15¼" up.

44 Bore all those mortises. The seat rung and seat rail mortises will intersect a bit, but cut both to their full depth, about 1⅞". Then remove the end blocks.

45 Cut the rungs, the seat support, and the seat and back rails to length, and cut tenons on both ends of all of them. Cut tenons on the bottom end of the four posts, too.

46 Split a curved sapling, 22" long and about 4½" diameter, in half for the two arms, and plane the split faces smooth. Chop away enough waste on the back ends of the arms so that you can cut tenons there.

47 Dry fit two rungs and two posts for each side. Measure from the front of the back posts to the centers of the front post tenons to determine where to drill mortises in the bottoms of the arms. Mark the arms, and bore the mortises, but avoid drilling right through. Dry fit the arms, and then disassemble the side panels.

48 Plane about ¼" from the top sides of the two seat rungs to form a flat area about 2" wide, as shown in figure 4. Apply epoxy to the mortises, and assemble the side panels, making sure that the flats on the top rungs are facing upward.

49 Mark the center, lengthwise, of the seat rails, and bore mortises for the seat

support. Dry fit the seat rails in the side panels, measure for the seat support, and cut it to length. Then cut tenons on both ends.

50 Plane a flat area on the seat support and the seat rails to match those on the seat rungs. All the flat areas should be in the same plane. Plane similar flats on the fronts of the back rails.

51 Dry fit the bench structure and, if it looks good, glue it together. You've got the flats for the seat up and the flats for the back in front, right?

52 Hold each suspension rail against the post tenons to mark for mortises, making sure they are centered lengthwise. Then bore the mortises, and glue the suspension rails in place.

53 If a local mill can supply cedar flitches for the seat and back, use those. Otherwise, you can use regular cedar lumber

Figure 4

with planed edges. Cut the seat and back slats to length. Cut the front seat slat to fit between the front posts.

54 Nail the seat slats in place first with a little space between them. Turn the bench on its back, and lay out the back slats. Nail them to the back rails with their bottom ends just above the seat slats.

55 Now install the swing hardware. Drill pilot holes in the ends of the suspension rails for screw eyes, and turn them in tight to the eye. Drill ⅜" holes vertically in the centers of the

outer collar ties, and install the hook bolts. Run a length of chain from each eye screw to a hook bolt, adjusting the height and slant of the bench.

56 With the bench at a comfortable height, consider how to trim the tops of the back slats. To match the curve of the truss rail, bend a skinny piece of wood, and hold it to the bench back with spring clamps. Adjust the curve until you like it, draw your line, and cut the curve with a jigsaw or handsaw. Sand the top ends of the back slats and you're finished. I'll bet a beer would taste real good right now, and I know where I'd drink it.

Figure 5

GALLERY
BY DANIEL MACK

This gallery of rustic outdoor work is a different kind of "how-to." This is the how to dream and wonder section. Collected here are examples of many different kinds of work that have provoked me to think about, and to reconsider, the ways and whys of rustic. Together they reflect the common pot, the stew of materials and ideas we all work out of. Most of them are made using the techniques introduced in Building with Sticks and in the projects. But, again, there is really no one right way of doing something rustic. Invention is always the essence of rustic making.

The Comfort of Utility

It's always safe in rustic to start with some simple need: "We need a fence over there... a trellis for that wisteria." Two-dimensional shapes are the most inviting to start with. They are fast and can be nailed, lashed, or fussed over in a woodworking way.

TOP: Grapevine fence, Nancy Weaver. *Photo by Nancy Weaver*

ABOVE: Leaf design gate, red cedar. *Photo by Daniel Mack*

ABOVE RIGHT: Fallen wood rail, Windel Dills, Waynesville, NC. *Photo by Daniel Mack*

RIGHT: Twig-lattice fence, Sharon Ladd, Yellowknife, NWT. *Photo by Sharon Ladd*

If you put a few flat pieces together, you get arbors:

Arbor, Nancy Weaver.
Photo by Nancy Weaver

Arbor in Winter, Tom Holmes,
Greeley, PA. *Photo by Tom Holmes*

Arbor, Romancing the Woods, Inc.,
Woodstock, NY, 1992. *Photo by Jan Schryburt*

Chairs and benches are a bit more complicated, but they are just flat panels connected together:

ABOVE: Driftwood chair built around a 3" slab of oak. *Photo by Bruce Cagwin*

LEFT: *Wild Wayside Bench*, James Roth. *Photo by James Roth*

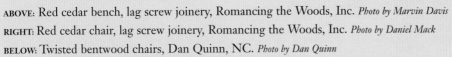

ABOVE: Red cedar bench, lag screw joinery, Romancing the Woods, Inc. *Photo by Marvin Davis*
RIGHT: Red cedar chair, lag screw joinery, Romancing the Woods, Inc. *Photo by Daniel Mack*
BELOW: Twisted bentwood chairs, Dan Quinn, NC. *Photo by Dan Quinn*

Structures

New York City's Central Park, built in the 1870's, was the first and most elaborate use of rustic in America. Parks in other cities then began to use rustic. Here is a selection of stereoscopic images from that period from the collection of art historian Charles Doherty.

These photos from the collection of Charles Doherty

In 1904, the rustic style was adopted as the theme of the National Park Service, and this inspired generations of public and private properties to follow suit. For instance, Mohonk Mountain House, in New Paltz, NY, has miles of walking trails with rustic "surprises."

ABOVE: Restaurant entrance, North Creek, NY.
Photo by Daniel Mack

RIGHT: At Mohonk Mountain House.
Photo by Daniel Mack

TOP CENTER: At Mohonk Mountain House.
Photo by Daniel Mack

TOP RIGHT: At Mohonk Mountain House.
Photo by Daniel Mack

Casual, Found, and Discovered: Rustic Lite?

Sometimes, all this designing and making seems just too much. Well, then it's time for Found and Discovered Rustic Work. The most fetching and primary form of rustic work is the simple pleasure of recognizing some pleasing shape, form, or texture.

Sometimes, rustic means simply discovering something in the woods and visiting it.

Ben Mozec
Photograph
Collection,
*University of Alaska,
Fairbanks*

Hollow Sycamore Shelter.
Photo by Daniel Mack

This found-shape man, called "Old Sourdough," greeted people outside a store in rural Alaska.

A chunk of fallen tree and an hour with a chain saw can result in an inviting rustic project.

Lakeside bench,
Cascade Lake,
Warwick, NY.
Photo by Daniel Mack

This casual approach to rustic has been practiced from the beginning of rustic in America. It was 1858 when a drawing of this rustic bench was first published, and 140 years later I happened to see this version of it.

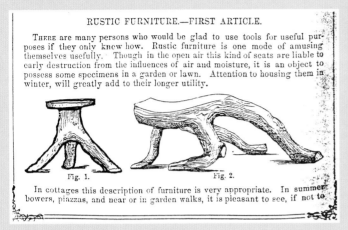

RUSTIC FURNITURE.—FIRST ARTICLE.

THERE are many persons who would be glad to use tools for useful purposes if they only knew how. Rustic furniture is one mode of amusing themselves usefully. Though in the open air this kind of seats are liable to early destruction from the influences of air and moisture, it is an object to possess some specimens in a garden or lawn. Attention to housing them in winter, will greatly add to their longer utility.

Fig. 1.   Fig. 2.

In cottages this description of furniture is very appropriate. In summer bowers, piazzas, and near or in garden walks, it is pleasant to see, if not to

Drawing in *The Horticulturist*, 1858

Yard bench, Block Island, RI, 1999. *Photo by Daniel Mack*

Sometimes, the bending, lashing, and stacking is rustic enough. These are the living quarters of the people at The Wilderness School in Brunswick, Maine.

Living Quarters,
The Wilderness School,
Brunswick, ME, 2000.
Photos by Daniel Mack

*For the last five years,
I've been playing with
the frisky forsythia in
my yard, "pleaching" it
into arbors and bowers.*

Living forsythia huts.
Photo by Daniel Mack

Some fences can be just collections of wood, like this one in Vincent Massaro's front yard in New York.

*Or this smaller one that Bernadette
Scutaro and I made with children in
an after-school program.*

ABOVE: *Photo by Daniel Mack*
LEFT: Stacked wood garden edging. *Photo by Daniel Mack*

Art, Garden Art, Yard Art, and Sculpture

Outside the realm of furniture, accessories, and structures, often a brave new voice can be heard. What it produces gets called yard art, outdoor sculpture, land art, or garden art. Remember that "art" is just a three-letter word that means "the things we all make."

Water Work, "California Pie," Roy Staab, 2000. *Photo by Roy Staab*

Chair for the Birds, grapevine, Nancy Weaver.
Photo by Nancy Weaver

Treework, Patrick Dougherty, Katonah Museum, Katonah, NY. *Photo by Daniel Mack*

Natural forms are not just building materials for projects.
They can also be the excuse that allows us to explore
the unruly territories of the imagination.

Stickball with Chair, The Garden Project, Vincent Massaro, Rochester, New York. *Photo by artist*

ACKNOWLEDGMENTS

Every published book results from collaborative effort, but this one benefited from extraordinary contributions by many people. We want to thank:

Andy Rae *for getting this project off the ground and gathering the projects;* **Deborah Morgenthal** *and* **Kathy Sheldon** *for applying firm but gentle editorial hands to the text, and Deborah again for her clear-eyed leadership and her facility with making the close calls;* **Celia Naranjo** *for creating a clear and lovely design;*

And especially **Frank Rohrbach** *for his patience and persistence while producing fine illustrations under difficult strictures; and* **Charlie Covington** *for turning a jumble of text and images into attractive pages with amazing speed and grace.*

CONTRIBUTING DESIGNERS

We want to thank the artists who designed and built the projects for this book. They generously provided photographs, drawings, and information, answered our questions, and contributed their creative energy. We appreciate their help and enthusiasm.

Greg Ani is inspired by the shapes and rugged appearance of northern willows, birch, and alder to create unique furniture and décor for living rooms, porches, gardens, and specialty shops. See his work at www.backwoodswillow.com, or email him at greg@backwoodswillow.com.

Kevin Barnes builds rustic indoor and outdoor furniture and art pieces in Asheville, North Carolina. He also creates outdoor sanctuary spaces. Reach him at 828-232-0953.

Susan Churchill designs and builds bent willow furnishings and garden structures through her business, Deertail Creek Furnishings, in Madison, Wisconsin. She also offers seasonal workshops. She can be reached at 608-257-3922 or deertailcreek@yahoo.com.

Joel Cole is a decorative artist specializing in murals and faux finishes in addition to his work in garden design. He can be contacted at joelcole@juno.com.

Brian Creelman designs and builds rustic furniture, garden structures and architectural accents throughout Eastern Canada and New England. He can be reached at customrustic@sympatico.ca.

Jim Cunningham creates simple but elegant rustic furnishings in his shop in Bristol, Vermont. View Jim's work at www.moosemaple.com.

Skip Davidson moved from an urban to a rural environment, from dust to clean air, and from furniture making to willow craft and rustic mythical woodcarving. He can be reached at Marsh Line Willow Works, RR2 West Lorne, Ontario, Canada N0L-2P0 or by phone at 519-768-1908.

Cheryl Evans creates a distinctive collection of rustic designs for the home and garden. View her work at www.magma.ca/~cevans, or contact her at cevans@magma.ca.

Tor Faegre makes furniture and sculpture out of twigs, branches, bark and steel in Evanston, Illinois. He can be reached at tornsue@aol.com.

Carla Filippelli creates and markets one-of-a-kind random weave baskets and sculptural weavings in her studio in Asheville, North Carolina. She can be reached at cranberrycreek@main.nc.us.

Greg Harkins makes rustic and turned chairs for "U.S. Presidents…and other big dogs, but mostly just Common Folk" at his shop in Vaughan, Mississippi. View his work at www.harkinschairs.com, or contact him at greg@harkinschairs.com.

Tammy M. Perrine owns and operates Rustic Class, specializing in traditional greenwood-joinery furniture with hickory bark seating in addition to natural bath and body products. Her work may be viewed at www.rusticclass.com or contact her at rusticclass@rtol.net.

Andy Rae has been writing about, designing, and making furniture for two decades. Formerly senior editor at *American Woodworker* magazine, he has written several books, including *The Complete Illustrated Guide to Furniture and Cabinet Construction* (2001, Taunton Press). Reach him at woodrae@aol.com.

Paul Ruhlmann is the primary inventor of the Veritas Tenon Cutter®. He has taught at Buckingham Browne & Nichols School in Cambridge, Massachusetts for 25 years. He also makes furniture and sculpture for gallery sales and private commissions. Contact him at paul_ruhlmann@bbns.org.

Laura Spector designs and builds custom rustic furnishings in the European Romantic tradition at her studio in Fairfield, Connecticut. She can be reached at www.lauraspectorrusticdesign.com, or by email at lsrustic@aol.com, or by phone at 203-254-3952.

Terry Taylor is an artist, designer, and jewelry maker, who creates numerous projects for Lark Books, as well as authoring craft books on different topics. He is currently writing a book for Lark on altered art.

Kim Vergil makes rustic furniture, garden accessories, and paintings in Baie d'Urfe, Quebec. She also teaches courses on rustic furniture and living chairs. View her work at www.kimcreations.net and email her at okvergil@videotron.ca.

Marcia Whitt creates rustic accessories, baskets, and furniture along with her husband, John. They live in rural north Missouri and can be reached at www.thebenttree.com.

PHOTO CREDITS

Greg Ani, p.114

Evan Bracken, pp.28, 30, 35, 36, 44, 46, 49, 53, 56, 71, 77, 92, 97, 104, 112, 113

Brian Creelman, p.124

Hélène Anne Fortin, pp.2, 3, 27, 40, 58, 99, 100, 109

William Gilmore, p.122

Thomas Loof, p.75

Daniel Mack, pp.6, 7, 16

Paul Ruhlmann, pp.118, 119

Thomas Stender, pp.1, 4, 14-26, 27, 39, 70

Kim Vergil, p.38, 67

Marcia Whitt, p.33

A NOTE ABOUT SUPPLIERS

Usually, the supplies you need for making the projects in Lark Books can be found at your local craft supply store, discount mart, home improvement center, or retail shop relevant to the topic of the book. Occasionally, however, you may need to buy materials or tools from specialty suppliers. In order to provide you with the most up-to-date information, we have created suppliers listings on our Web site, which we update on a regular basis. Visit us at www.larkbooks.com, click on "Craft Supply Sources," and then click on the relevant topic. You will find numerous companies listed with their web address and/or mailing address and phone number.

INDEX

Metrics Conversion Formulas		
U.S. Length	**Multiply By**	**Metric**
Inch	2.54	Centimeters
Foot	0.3048	Meters
Yard	0.9144	Meters